MILK-ANALYSIS.

A PRACTICAL TREATISE

ON THE

EXAMINATION OF MILK AND ITS DERIVATIVES,
CREAM, BUTTER, AND CHEESE.

BY

J. ALFRED WANKLYN, M.R.C.S.,

CORRESPONDING MEMBER OF THE ROYAL BAVARIAN ACADEMY OF SCIENCES;
PUBLIC ANALYST FOR BUCKINGHAMSHIRE, BUCKING-
HAM, ANG HIGH WYCOMBE.

NEW YORK:
D. VAN NOSTRAND, PUBLISHER.
23 MURRAY AND 27 WARREN STREET
1874.

PREFACE.

—:o:—

During the year 1871 I devoted much attention to the subject of milk-analysis, and, besides making many hundreds of analyses of milk purchased in different parts of London for the *Milk Journal*, was employed by Government in an investigation into the milk supplied to the Metropolitan Workhouses. I have likewise examined the milk supplied to the Hospitals in London.

In the course of this work, I have been fortunate enough to make some improvements in the art of milk-analysis, and, in particular, some little modifications in the taking of milk-residues, so as to tranfer such determinations (which before were tedious and uncertain) into the list of the simplest and most exact of chemical analyses. At the present time, when a new class of men has been constituted to watch over the food of the country, there is need for special manuals of this description.

LONDON, *November*, 1873.

CONTENTS.

MILK-ANALYSIS.

CHAPTER I.

INTRODUCTORY.

MILK, which is the secretion of the mammary glands, and constitutes the entire food and drink of the young mammal, is an aqueous solution of caseine, milk-sugar, and small quantities of mineral material, and holds in suspension a quantity of fat in a state of fine subdivision.

The milk of the cow, to which we will confine our attention in this work, has been analyzed at various times by many chemists. My own analyses, which are among the most recent, are as follows :—

In 100 cubic centimetres of average country milk I found—

Water	90.09	grammes.
Fat	3.16	"
Caseine	4.16	"
Milk-sugar . . .	4.76	"
Ash	0.73	"
	102.90	

Town-fed milk is a little richer. According to my analysis, it contains in 100 cubic centimetres—

Water	88.43	grammes.
Fat	4.12	"
Caseine	5.16	"
Milk-sugar	4.43	"
Ash	0.76	"
	102.90	

I have likewise made an analysis of the milk of the Alderney cow, which, notwithstanding the popular prejudice in its favor, as will be seen, does not much differ from other milk. I found in 100 cubic centimetres of such milk—

Water	89.88	grammes.
Fat	3.31	"
Caseine	4.75	"
Milk-sugar	4.24	"
Ash	0.72	"
	102.90	

The water which enters into the constitution of milk may be extracted from it by evaporation, and, that having been done, there will remain behind the *milk solids*, which consist of the fat, caseine, milk-sugar, and ash (or mineral matters) conjointly.

The fat exists in milk in the form of very minute globules. It is not a single chemical substance, but a mixture of chemical substances. It consists of olein, palmitin, stearin, and small quantities of butyrin and other fats. All these different fatty substances are ethers of glycerine, and are capable of yielding glycerine when digested with alkalies, yielding as the same time the corresponding alkaline salt. Thus when the fat of milk is digested with potash or soda, it furnishes glycerine, and, at the same time, the oleate, palmitate, stearate, and butyrate of potash or soda. The fat of milk is hard at winter temperatures, and soft at summer temperatures (its fusing point lying, in fact, at such temperatures as are reached in summer). Fat is distinguished from the other solid constituents of milk by being soluble in ether.

Caseine.—This is the nitrogenous constituent of milk. In regard to this portion of the milk, the remark should first be made that it is not perfectly homogeneous—that is to say, there are at least two distinct chemical substances comprised by the nitrogenous portion of milk.

There is caseine proper, and also albumen—that is to say, a certain proportion of the nitrogenous substance is coagulated on boiling milk, but the major part of the nitrogenous substance is not coagulated on boiling. Whether the portion of nitrogenous substance which is not coagulated on boiling is itself homogeneous, is even a matter of some doubt. In a corresponding case—that of flour—we know that the nitrogenous constituent is a very complex mixture, and that, under the name of gluten, a whole tribe of substances are comprehended. Under the name of caseine it will be convenient to designate the entire nitrogenous constituents of milk; just as, under the name gluten, the entire nitrogenous portion of flour is comprehended. Like albumen, caseine exists under two modifications—it is either soluble or insoluble. In the former of these states it exists in fresh milk; in the latter, after the milk has "turned."

It used to be believed that the soluble variety of caseine was in reality a salt caseine, wherein caseine played the part of acid, and the alkali naturally present in milk-ash played the part of base. The coagulation or curdling of milk was explained on the supposition that lactic acid, generated by incipient fermentation of the milk-sugar, decomposed this hypothetical compound, and threw down insoluble caseine.

This explanation must be abandoned, inasmuch as investigation has shown that the ash of milk is almost absolutely devoid of alkali. In truth, we are driven to the conclusion, that the change from soluble to insoluble caseine is molecular, resembling the change from soluble silica to insoluble silica.

The ultimate composition of caseine is not distinguishable from that of albumen and fibrine, viz.—

Carbon	53.7
Hydrogen	7.1
Nitrogen	15.7
Oxygen	23.5
	100.0

There is likewise a trace of sulphur, said to be about one per cent. In milk the caseine is chemically combined with phosphate of lime; and there is no known method of effecting a separation between the two without destroying the caseine.

Milk is coagulated—that is to say, the caseine is rendered insoluble—by the action of rennet, of acid, and of many metallic salts.

Caseine which has become insoluble in water is redissolved by alkalis, and also by solution of phosphate of soda.

Milk-sugar, $C_{12}H_{22}O_{11}H_2O$.—This substance may be obtained from milk by coagulating the caseine and removing that along with the fat, and then evaporating the residual liquid (or whey) to crystallization. The crystals are decolorized by means of animal charcoal. It is distinguished from cane-sugar in various ways.

In composition. When dried at 100° Cent., milk-sugar has the formula as given above, viz., $C_{12}H_{22}O_{11}H_2O$; cane-sugar, on the contrary, when dried at 100° Cent., exhibits the composition $C_{12}H_{22}O_{11}$. Heated to about 140° Cent., milk-sugar loses an atom of water, and becomes $C_{12}H_{22}O_{11}$.

In solubility in water there is much difference between the two. Milk-sugar dissolves in five or six parts of cold water and in two and a half parts of boiling water. Cane sugar, on the other hand, is far more soluble. It dissolves in one third of its volume of cold water, and in exceedingly little boiling water.

Milk-sugar is not so heavy as cane-sugar, its specific gravity being 1.53; whilst cane-sugar has a specific gravity of 1.606.

Towards alkaline-copper-solution, the behavior of the two kinds of sugar is quite different; whereas milk-sugar reduces the oxide to the suboxide of copper even in the cold, solution of cane-sugar does not even effect a reduction on being heated to the boiling point of water.

The Ash, or Mineral Matter.—When milk is dried up, and the dried residue afterwards incinerated, the ash remains behind. This consists mainly of phosphate of lime, which forms about two-thirds of it, and of chlorides. There is hardly any free or carbonated alkali in the ash of cow's milk. The degree of freedom of the ash from alkali may be judged of from the fact, ascertained by myself, that the ash does not neutralize as much standard acid as it would if one hundredth of its weight consisted of alkaline-carbonate.

Such, then, are the component parts of milk. It remains to be added, that milk has a specific gravity of about 1.029, at 15.6 C., and that its physical appearance is very peculiar. It is not a clear liquid, being, in point of fact, an emulsion. Left to itself, it by and by becomes surmounted with a whitish layer, well known as cream. When fresh, it is very nearly neutral to test-paper, but is very apt to turn sour from very slight causes.

Milk exhibits great constancy of composition; the effect of variations in the diet of the cow showing itself in the amount of the secretion rather than in its quality. This is very strikingly manifested on making a comparison of the milk yielded by the poor and ill-fed Bengali cow in India with that given by our own highly-fed beasts in this country. Dr. Macnamara's analyses of the milk of the Bengali cows show that it hardly differs from the milk of English cows in quality, whereas in quantity it differs greatly, the yield of milk from the former being a small fraction only of that from the latter. The milk of an animal has probably very much the same constancy of composition as the blood of the animal. It is well known that, by administering water to an animal, we are not able to dilute its blood to any considerable extent. Instead of telling on the blood, the water tells on the perspiration or on the urine, so that from containing four or five per cent. of solids, the urine may become so dilute as to contain only one per cent. of solids. The milk resembles the blood in this respect, and is in contrast with the urine; and by giving an animal an excess of water we do not dilute its milk, but its urine.

As will be readily comprehended, this constancy of composition is a cardinal fact in milk analysis. If milk were variable in strength, as urine is, chemical analysis would fail to detect the watering of milk. That milk is a secretion of constant, or only slightly varying composition, lies at the very root of the subject of this treatise.

In Chapter IX., on "*The Milk Supply of the London Workhouses*," the experimental evidence bearing upon this question is minutely entered into.

CHAPTER II.

INSTRUMENTS AND METHODS FOR TESTING MILK—OUTLINE OF MILK-ANALYSIS.

THE *lactometer*, or *lactodensimeter*, as it has been called, to distinguish it from another simple instrument, the cream-ometer, was at one time a great favorite. In France, a few years ago, if not indeed now, the police would take action at once on a reading of that instrument, and turn milk out into the gutter if it were condemned. And in London, the lactometer is exposed for sale in shop windows, and both the public and milk dealers trust to it. Even in some recent manuals intended for the guidance of medical officers of health, the use of the lactometer is recommended. In one of them in particular—Dr. Edward Smith's—which claims a sort of pseudo-government sanction, the lactometer is very prominently put forward, and commended as being for milk what the hydrometer is for alcoholic fluids.

But, although it is so very popular, and although it has been so implicitly trusted, the lactometer is a most untrust-worthy instrument. There hardly ever was an instrument which has so utterly failed as the lactometer. It confounds together milk which is exceptionally rich with milk which has been largely watered; and many a poor French peasant, bringing the best and unadulterated produce of his dairy into a French town, has been ruthlessly stopped by the police, who have dipped their lactometer into the milk, and forthwith sent it down the gutter, as if it had been milk and water.

Very curious things, too, are done in this country by reason of trust in the lactometer. There is a prison not far from London, and the prison authorities are specially particular about their supply of milk. They allow no milk to enter the prison unless it comes up to the M. mark on a certain lactometer. The M. mark is pitched very high, and the milk purveyor reaches the M. mark by skimming the milk.

A very little consideration will suffice to make intelligible the obliquity of the indications of the lactometer, and to show how untrustworthy it must be. The lactometer, as of course will be understood, is simply the hydrometer applied to milk; and readings of the instrument are neither more nor less than specific gravities. The more milk-sugar and caseine and mineral matter there is in a given specimen of milk, the greater (other things being equal) will be its density or specific gravity, and the higher the lactometer reading.

If, however, fat globules (as happens in the instance of milk) be diffused through the fluid, then, because fat is lighter than water, the effect of the other milk solids on the gravity of the liquid will be more or less neutralized. The density of milk-fat is about 0.9, water being 1.0. Now, if a solution of caseine and milk-sugar, of specific gravity 1.030, be sufficiently charged with fat globules, its specific gravity may be sent down even below the gravity of water. How much would be required to bring about such a result is a matter of simple calculation.

This being understood, it will be obvious, that if the specimens of milk differ in specific gravity, there must be two distinct and equally valid ways of accounting for the difference. The milk with the lower gravity may be milk let down with water, or let down with fat, *i. e.*, milk let down by being enriched.

By way of example, I would just refer to the specific gravity of the so-called strippings, which are the last portions of milk wrung out of the udder at the termination of the milking. These are richer in cream than the average mass of the milk, and they have a much lower density than average milk.

I have myself examined strippings with a specific gravity of 1.020, and a specific gravity of 1.025 is by no means uncommon. In the instance of strippings of the latter gravity, I found the percentage of solids to be 18.74.

Now, if we all knew concerning a sample of milk was that its gravity was 1.025, we might with equal reasonableness conclude, either that it contained fifteen or twenty per cent. of extraneous water, or that it was surcharged with cream.

If, by adding fat to milk, the specific gravity is lowered, it follows that by substracting fat (*i. e.*, by skimming), the specific gravity is raised; and hence the explanation of the reaching of the high M. mark by skimming.

A certain trick of the milk trade is fostered by the employment of the lactometer. The milk is partially denuded of cream (accomplished conveniently by adding a certain quantity of skimmed milk to the fresh milk), and thereby raised in gravity. That being accomplished, it is dosed with water, and its gravity is thereby lowered to the normal standard.

Let no one think that he would discover such a trick by making an estimation of cream; for watered milk throws up its fat in the form of cream more perfectly than unwatered milk.

Another objection relative to the lactometer (which, however, pertains to the application of the hydrometer to organic fluids generally) is drawn from the circumstance that a comparatively small change in density corresponds to a great change in composition. Making total abstraction of the difficulty and uncertainty dependent on the cream, and regarding milk as a solution of caseine and milk-sugar, it will be seen that whereas the specific gravity of water rises only from 1.000 to 1.032 in passing into milk, the water receives 9.2 per cent. of milk solids. In other words, while the density goes up only three per cent., the solids go up nine per cent. It is, therefore, disadvantageous to estimate rise in solid content by rise in density. Mineral substances, when they dissolve in water, raise the density far more rapidly than organic substances. The contrast in this respect is very well shown when chloride of potassium is compared with milk solids. Thus, a ten per cent. solution of chloride of potassium has a specific gravity of 1.065 at 15° Cent., whereas a ten per cent. solution of caseine and milk-sugar has a specific gravity of about 1.035.

To be of any value at all, a specific gravity determination in the case of such a fluid as milk must be taken with extreme accuracy; and, as is well known, the taking of specific gravities with great accuracy is not by any means one of the most facile of operations, and is certainly not easier than the taking of solid residues directly.

From a careful consideration of the whole subject, I am convinced that one of the most necessary steps to be taken in milk analysis is to abandon the use of the lactometer.

The creamometer is a graduated tube, in which milk is allowed to stand and throw up cream, the volume of which is afterwards to be read.

It is, of course, unnecessary for the graduation to be continued throughout the whole extent of the tube. If the graduation be prolonged only for the uppermost fifteen per cent., that will be amply sufficient for all practical purposes—*vide* fig.

Normal milk yields about ten per cent. of cream; but that is subject to great irregularity, and a milk may yield very much less without having been tampered with, or it may yield the ten per cent., and, nevertheless, have been tampered with. As will be explained in the chapter devoted to cream, that fluid is subject to great variations in richness. The creamometer is at best a treacherous guide.

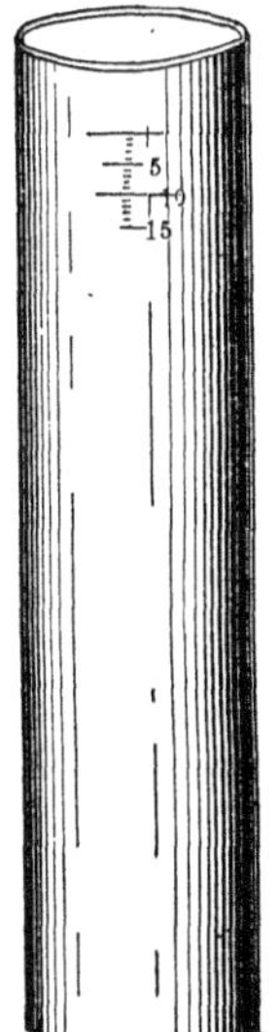

In addition to the lactometer and the creamometer, there is likewise an instrument, the indications of which depend upon the degree of opacity produced by the fat globules. It is an instrument which I have never tried, and which, indeed, does not promise much.

The only really safe and satisfactory manner of examining milk is by means of an analysis of it. This used to be considered a long and tedious, and little satisfactory operation. By the aid of a few simple devices, milk analysis may be very much simplified. The first step to be taken is to determine the milk solids, and, of course, the water, which is the difference between the solids and the quantity of milk which yields them. The detail of this operation will be given in next chapter. After having determined the milk solids, the fat is next to be determined. If the amount of fat be subtracted from the amount of milk solids, the amount of "solids not fat" will be arrived at. A knowledge of this datum is (as will be explained) sufficient to enable a judgment to be come to as to whether or not the sample of milk has been watered.

As a rule, an examination of milk, which has proceeded thus far, is complete. If only watering or skimming, or both, had taken place, the examination would have been ample.

The determinations of caseine and of milk-sugar are useful when the question arises of other possible adulteration. The determination of ash is made with a view of ascertaining the presence of extraneous mineral matter. It has the merit of being very easy of execution. A highly-watered milk will obviously, as one of its characters, show too low an ash. In the following chapters we shall describe in detail the method of arriving at each of these data.

CHAPTER III.

MILK-SOLIDS.

THE first step in dealing with a sample of milk is to insure that it is thoroughly mixed up. This is most conveniently done by pouring it from one vessel to another; and it is essential to attend to this particular in order to avoid getting either too much or too little cream—that is to say, either a greater or less proportion than the sample really contains. It is also well, in this preliminary stage of the inquiry, to make out whether the milk be sour or not, and whether or not it be curdled. If very sour, there is of course a chance of destruction of some of the organic material, and the degree of acidity in such a case ought to be measured by means of standard solution of alkali. If the milk be curdled, care will also have to be taken to avoid an unequal distribution of the caseine; and in cases of this kind, I do not like to use the pipette for measuring off the quantity of milk, but I prefer to weigh out the quantity of milk taken for analysis.

Assuming that the milk is fresh and in good condition, it may be measured in a small pipette—*vide* fig.

The quantity taken for analysis is five cubic centimetres. Pipettes for the discharge of 5 c. c. may be purchased of Messrs. Townson & Mercer, who supply them graduated very satisfactorily. The pipette should be accurate, within $\frac{2}{100}$ of a cubic centimetre; and should be tested by being charged with water, and discharged into a counterpoised beaker or flask, which, with its contents, is to be weighed. The discharged water should not differ from 5 grammes by more than 0.02 grammes.

In order to be able to take milk-solids, the experimenter requires—

1. A balance.
2. Small platinum dishes.
3. Water bath.
4. Pipette.

If a good chemical balance and weights be at hand, so much the better. If not, and the question arise relative to the least practicable expenditure in the matter of balance, the following information may possibly be acceptable.

I have seen a balance made by Becker & Sons, of New York, and Kruiskady, Rotterdam,* which indicates two milligrammes quite distinctly when loaded with fifty grammes, and which costs £2. This balance, which is No. 14 on Messrs. Becker & Sons' published catalogue, will answer very well. For weights, it is essential to have a good set, and the box costing 30s. will be required.

If 5 c. c. of milk be taken, it will be obvious that an error of five milligrammes equals 0.1 gramme per 100 c. c.; and with a balance and weights and pipette, such as just mentioned, there should be no difficulty in getting determinations of residue which are not more than a few hundredths per cent. off the truth. The evaporation to dryness is most conveniently performed in a small platinum dish weighing some twelve grammes, and of the size figured.

If there be many milks to examine, it will be well to have a set of the little dishes (which cost 14s. a piece, and which are numbered on the lip). The dishes are to be cleaned and

* Mr. Henry Gillman, 143 Brecknock Road, London, N., is sole agent in England.

weighed, and the weights noted down; they will alter in weight only very slowly, and even if in active use, require reweighing only every now and then.

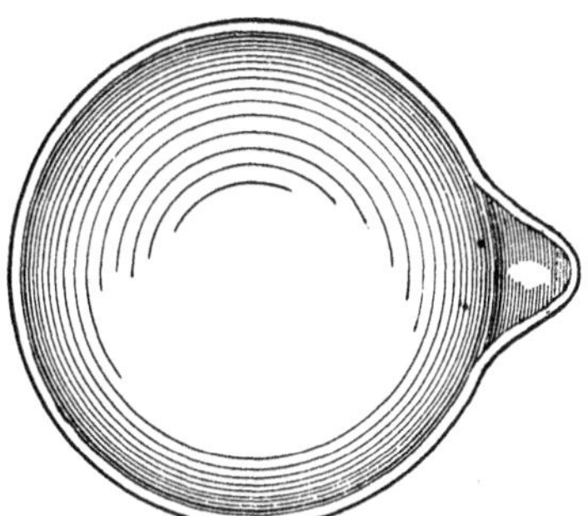

The dishes are conveniently heated in an oblong copper bath, with round holes cut in the top to receive them. The bath should be some six inches deep, and is charged with water. It is conveniently supported on a tripod, and heated with a Bunsen burner.

The dishes having been weighed, placed in order in the bath, and each one having received its charge of 5 c. c. of milk, the water in the bath is to be made to boil vigorously, and maintained boiling for three hours. At the expiration of that period the 5 c. c. of milk in each dish will have completely dried up. Each dish, with its contents, is removed from the bath, its outside is wiped, and itself and contents forthwith weighed.

The weight of the dish subtracted from the weight of conjoined dish and contents leaves the weight of the milk-solids given by the 5 c. c. of milk. By multiplying that weight by 20, the yield from 100 c. c. of milk is arrived at. If care be taken in this operation, results may be obtained which differ from one another by only a small figure in the second decimal place in percentage.

When I first worked this process, I employed a pipette which discharged, not 5 c. c., but 5 grammes of milk, of average density; and in that way obtained results which, multiplied by 20, expressed percentage. I have, however, come to the conclusion, that it is better to express the result, not exactly in percentage, but in grammes yielded by 100 c. c. of milk, and that mode of statement I am now in the habit of adopting.

As before said, if the milk be curdled, it is not well to use the pipette, and to take the 5 c. c., but to weigh out an irregular quantity of the milk (about 5 grammes), and dry it up.

The following examples will serve to illustrate the degree of accuracy easily attainable by this process.

A sample of good country milk was submitted to the process four times, with the following results:—

	MILK.		MILK-SOLIDS.
I.	4.969 grammes gave	.	0.616 grammes.
II.	5.0105 " "	.	0.6255 "
III.	5.007 " "	.	0.623 "
IV.	5.0145 " "	.	0.626 "

Expressed in percentage, this is equivalent to—

MILK.		MILK-SOLIDS.
100 grammes gave	. .	12.40 grammes.
" " "	. .	12.48 "
" " "	. .	12.44 "
" " "	. .	12.48 "
and the mean,	. .	12.45 "

A specimen of rich town-fed milk yielded in four experiments—

	MILK.	MILK-SOLIDS.
I.	5.000 grammes gave	0.7035 grammes.
II.	5.004 " "	0.705 "
III.	5.000 " "	0.7025 "
IV.	5.006 "	0.705 "

Or in percentage—

MILK.	MILK-SOLIDS.
100 grammes gave . .	14.07 grammes.
" " " . .	14.09 "
" " " . .	14.05 "
" " " . .	14.08 "
and the mean, . .	14.07 "

These are not exceptionally carefully done, and only illustrate the degree of accuracy which is attainable by the most ordinary care.

In conclusion, it remains to add, that such results are not to be expected if the residues be weighed before the expiration of the prescribed time—viz., the three hours—and that the water in the bath must be kept boiling vigorously the whole time. By prolonging the drying for a second period of three hours, no sensible diminution takes place in the milk-solids.

The employment of plaster of paris or sand (both of which have been recommended for the purpose of rendering milk residues porous), is to be avoided. When only five cubic centimetres of milk are taken, as has been recommended in this chapter, it is likewise unnecessary to stir up the milk during the evaporation and drying.

CHAPTER IV.

THE FAT.

THE fat in milk is estimated by dissolving it in ether (which dissolves it, but does not dissolve any other constituent of milk), and evaporating the ethereal solution to dryness, and weighing the dried residue. It is not practicable to apply the ether directly to the milk itself, but the ether must be applied to the dry milk-solids.

The residue obtained, as described in last chapter, by evaporating and drying up 5 c. c. of milk, may be taken for the determination of the fat.

This residue, as will be understood, is contained in a small platinum dish. Ether is to be poured into the dish, and heated to the boiling point, and poured out through a small filter. This operation of boiling and pouring off the ethereal solution must be repeated at least three times, and care is required to let none of the fat make its escape over the bottom of the dish. The filter should be large enough to avoid the chance of spilling the ethereal solution as it is being poured on to the filter. It is advisable to wash the bottom of the little platinum dish with ether, in order to avoid all chance of loss. Attention must also be paid to the filter-paper after the ether has passed through it. Of course it will require washing with ether; and after the residual ether has evaporated off, will be found with a little rim of fat surmounting it. This is best dealt with by cutting it off, and macerating it with a fresh portion of ether, which may then be rapidly poured through a second small filter. In order to facilitate the solution of the fat, the milk residue may be first moistened with alcohol, which will tend to disintegrate it, and favor the action of the ether upon it.

With regard to the quality of the ether employed, it should be tolerably dry; but it may be methylated ether. Of course it should leave no appreciable residue when 50 c. c. of it are evaporated and dried in the water-bath. The cost of such ether is about 16s. per gallon, and the cost of the ether consumed in each determination of fat is not more than twopence. I would, however, give the advice to be liberal with the ether; for it is false economy to ruin the determination for the sake of saving ether.

As will be apparent on trying practically to make these determinations of fat, the yield from 5 c. c. of milk is rather inconveniently small. I prefer to take 10 c. c. of milk, and to evaporate down in a larger platinum dish. A dish capable of holding 40 c. c., which costs about 30s., will answer very well. A small platinum spatula may be inserted into the milk, and used to stir it up occasionally during the evaporation. In this instance, it is unnecessary to push the drying of the milk-solids to completeness, and an hour's evaporation in the water-bath is amply sufficient for the purpose. Just at last, the milk residue should be moistened with alcohol to soften it. The mode of dissolving out the fat with ether, and the passing of the ethereal solution through the filter, and the subsequent treatment of the residual rim of fat in the filter paper, has been already explained.

The ethereal solution of fat having been obtained (and, by the way, it ought never to be less than 50 c. c.), the next point to be attended to is the evaporation of the ether, and the getting of the residue of fat.

In laboratories where there is a platinum dish capable of holding 100 c. c., such as is used in taking water residues, that may be employed for the purpose of containing the solution.

The dish having been weighed, is charged with the ethereal solution, and placed in warm water, whereupon the evaporation of the ether may be made to proceed gently. As the evaporation approaches its termination, a change will be visible in the aspect of the solution. It will become turbid, owing to the trace of water and small quantity of

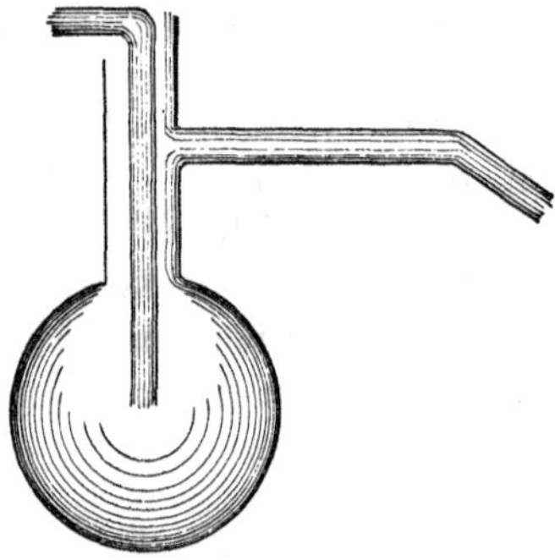

alcohol, which gradually predominate over the ether, being incapable of dissolving the fat. When this stage is reached, the dish should be transferred to the water-bath, and heated to 100° C. After being maintained at 100° C. for a short time, the solution will again become clear, owing to the evaporation of the trace of water and alcohol. When this clearness has come on, the fat is dry, and the dish may be removed from the bath, wiped, cooled, and, along with its contents, weighed. The weight of the empty dish being subtracted, the difference is the weight of the fat yielded by the milk. This multiplied by 10 or 20, as the case may be, gives the number of grammes of fat yielded by 100 c. c. of milk.

If it be desired to recover the ether, the evaporation may be managed in a small retort—*vide* fig.

In such a case, the empty retort should be first weighed, and subsequently the retort charged with the dry fat is to be weighed. It will further be necessary to send a stream of dry air through the retort towards the end of the operatio n

I do not, however, think that a saving of two or three pence, the value of the ether, is a sufficient inducement to cause the analyst to complicate his apparatus. The avoidance of disengagement of ether vapor into the laboratory may, however, under some circumstances, be a reason for adopting an arrangement of this description.

In general, a milk analysis is complete when milk solids and fat have been taken. If the latter be subtracted from the former, a very important datum—viz., *milk-solids not fat*—is arrived at. This datum, which is the most constant quantity in milk analysis, gives, by a very simple calculation, the extent of watering to which the milk has been subjected.

CHAPTER V.

CASEINE.

UNDER the title of caseine—perhaps it would be better to say crude caseine—I mean to designate the entire nitrogenous material of milk.

After the dry milk-solids have been got, and after the fat has been washed out of them by means of ether, as was explained at length in the last chapter, there remain behind the caseine, the milk-sugar, and the ash. By extracting with strong alcohol, and ultimately adding a little boiling water, so as in effect to extract, with very weak hot alcohol, the milk-sugar and the soluble part of the ash, *i. e*, the chlorides, will pass into solution. The caseine which remains behind is washed off the filter-paper into a little platinum dish, and dried up in the water-bath till it ceases to lose weight. It is weighed along with the containing vessel, and then ignited, and the weight of the vessel and adherent ash (phosphate of lime) subtracted from it. As has been already remarked, the phosphate of lime exists really in a state of chemical combination with the caseine in milk. The quantity of milk recommended for the estimation of fat—viz., 10 grammes—is suitable for the determination of the caseine. Of course, if the product of the operation be multiplied by 10, the quantity of caseine yielded by 100 c. c. of milk will be arrived at.

Another method of procedure, which is very generally recommended, but which I do not like so well as that just described, consists in taking a considerable quantity of milk

—say 50 or 100 c. c. of milk—and, without any preliminary evaporation to dryness, precipitating the caseine, which is to be washed with water, alcohol, and ether, and then to be dried and weighed. The precipitation is effected by warming the milk, and acidulating it with almost any common acid; either hydrochloric or sulphuric, or even ascetic acid will do. As aforesaid, I do not like that modification so well as the one first given.

A very different method of determining caseine in milk consists in measuring it by the albuminoid ammonia which it is capable of furnishing. This is certainly the quickest process, and is very satisfactory.

In order to practise it, the milk must first be diluted with a known volume of water, so that one volume of dilute milk may contain accurately $\frac{1}{100}$ of a volume of milk. This is conveniently accomplished by measuring out with the pipette 10 c. c. of milk, and dropping it into the litre flask, which is subsequently filled up to the litre mark. Or, of course, 5 c. c. of milk may be diluted to 500 c. c.

It is not necessary to use distilled water for the purpose, inasmuch as the error introduced by ordinary river or town water is inappreciable. The quantity of the diluted milk which is required for experiment is 5 or 10 cubic centimetres, equivalent to $\frac{5}{100}$ or $\frac{10}{100}$ of a cubic centimetre of real milk.

The mode of operation is as follows:—

Ten grammes of solid potash and 0.4 gramme of crystals of permanganate of potash are boiled with about half a litre of water, the whole being contained by a retort provided with a tubulure, and connected with a Liebig's condenser. The liquid is allowed to distil, and successive portions of distillate tested for ammonia. So soon as water begins to distil over in a state of freedom from ammonia, the portion of diluted milk is to be introduced into the retort through the tubulure.

The distillates which subsequently come over are charged with the ammonia arising from the destruction of the caseine.

The ammonia is to be measured by means of the Nessler test, which is now very well known. The details of the measurement of ammonia will be understood by all persons who are in the habit of working the water process of Wanklyn, Chapman, and Smith, and it is unnecessary to enter into them here.

Every one part by weight of caseine gives, treated in this manner, 0.065 part of ammonia. The yield of "albuminoid ammonia" from 100 c. c. of genuine milk is 0.26 grammes.

It is only by persons who work the ammonia process of water-analysis, and only in laboratories where arrangements are made for that process, that the convenience of this determination of caseine will be appreciated.

CHAPTER VI.

MILK-SUGAR.

After the milk-solids have been deprived of fat by means of ether, as explained in Chapter IV., they may be made to yield up the milk-sugar, if they be treated with alcohol and hot water. This has been explained in the preceding chapter.

It remains here to follow the weak alcoholic solution after its passage through the filter on which the caseine had been deposited. The solution is to be evaporated to dryness in the water-bath, and the residue adherent to the vessel in which the evaporation is performed, is to be weighed along with its containing vessel.

That having been done, it is ignited gently, and the residue on ignition subtracted from the total weight before ignition. The difference is the yield of milk-sugar. Multiply this by 10, and the number of grammes of milk-sugar yielded by 100 cubic centimetres of milk is found. With some chemists, a titration of milk-sugar, by means of copper solution, is in great favor. For this purpose 50 or 60 c. c. of milk are gently warmed and mixed with a little acetic acid in order to precipitate the caseine, which is separated by means of a filter. The filtrate is used in the titration in the following manner:—It is first diluted with nine times its volume of water, so that one litre contains the milk-sugar of 100 c. c. of milk. A measured quantity of standard copper-solution is then placed in a white basin, and diluted with four times its volume of water, and heated to boiling. Into it, whilst boiling, is dropped the above-mentionel diluted milk, previously acidulated and filtered. As the dilute milk drops from a burette, it instantly reduces the boiling copper-solution, which deposits red oxide of copper. The dropping is to be continued until the boiling copper-solution ceases to be reduced—until it is exhausted. The point of exhaustion is determined *roughly*, by observing when the blue color leaves the solution, and *finely*, by observing the exact point at which ferrocyanide of potassium ceases to strike a red color with the filtered solution, which must be slightly acidulated with acetic acid before being tested with the ferrocyanide. The standard copper-solution is prepared by dissolving 34.65 grammes of crystals of sulphate of copper in 200 c. c. of water. To this solution is added a solution made by dissolving 173 grammes of double tartrate of potash and soda in 480 c. c. of caustic soda solution, of specific gravity 1.14. The whole is diluted till it occupies the volume of one litre.

The standard solution, so prepared, is of such a strength that 10 c. c. are equivalent to 0.067 grammes of milk-sugar (dry at 100° C.)

I am not in the habit of using this process, but without doubt it is occasionally of value.

CHAPTER VII.

ASH.

If the milk-solids be ignited, the organic matter is destroyed, and the inorganic matter or ash remains behind. The operation is managed in a very simple manner. The small platinum dish containing the milk-solids from 5 c. c. of milk is placed on a small triangle, either of platinum, or of iron-wire, or of iron-wire covered with tobacco-pipe. The last mentioned is an admirable form of support, and is very well known to chemists. The flame, either of a spirit-lamp, or of a Bunsen burner, is then made to play upon the platinum dish. By and by the organic matter is burnt up, and a grey ash remains behind. The platinum dish and its contents are then allowed to cool, and weighed. After subtracting the weight of the dish, the weight of the ash remains. This, multiplied by 20, equals the number of grammes of ash or mineral matter contained by 100 c. c. of milk.

The importance of a determination of ash depends upon the fact that the correctness of it at once answers the question whether or not the milk has been adulterated with chalk, salt, or other inorganic impurity. I have made hundreds of determinations of ash, and not yet come across a single case of adulteration of this kind.

As will be seen on looking back, the quantity of ash contained by 100 c. c of milk is between 0.7 and 0.8 grammes. Now, suppose the milk to be watered--with, say London water. In such a case the ash would be diminished, inasmuch as 100 c. c. of London water contains only 0.03 grammes of mineral matter, whilst 100 c. c. of milk contains 0.73 grammes of mineral matter. Watering will, therefore, be indicated by diminished ash; and in cases of watering, it is worth while to make a careful determination of ash as a sort of confirmatory test.

CHAPTER VIII.

CALCULATION AND STATEMENT OF RESULTS.

THROUGHOUT the foregoing chapters, the mode of statement recommended has been to reckon the milk by measure in cubic centimetres, and the products—the milk-solids or fat, &c.—in grammes. This form of statement will be found to be the most convenient, involving, as it does, the least possible calculation.

Occasionally, however, as in the case of sour milk, we are compelled to weigh the milk instead of measuring it.

In such a case, a simple calculation will reduce the percentage statement into a statement in the prescribed form, *i. e.*, of how many grammes are yielded by 100 c. c. of milk. If the specific gravity of the sample of milk be known, the reduction consists in simply multiplying by the specific gravity; if the specific gravity be unknown, the milk should be assumed to be of average specific gravity, viz., 1.029, and the calculation made accordingly.

In milk-analysis there are two kinds of statement in use, viz, percentage statement—how much of any constituent of milk is contained by 100 parts of milk; and the other kind of statement, how many grammes of any constituent are contained by 100 cubic centimetres of milk. Inasmuch as 100 c. c. of average milk weighs 102.9 grammes, this second statement approximates to a statement of parts per 102.9 parts.

In the next chapter, which is a reprint from the *Chemical*

News, the form of statement is percentage, and the various data would be reduced to the other measure by multiplication by 1.029.

Having cleared away any confusion arising from this slight difference in scale, we pass on to consider the practical use to be made of the various data afforded by milk-analysis.

As will be remembered, 100 c. c. of milk of average quality contains 12.81 grammes of milk-solids. Very rich—exceptionally rich—stall-fed milk contains 14.47 grammes of milk-solids. Now, it must be obvious to every one, that very rich milk, let down with a little water, will stimulate milk of average quality.

There is a certain limit below which the milk of well-fed cows is never known to fall. Below 11.8 grammes of solids per 100 c. c., milk has not been known to fall.

The most variable constituent of milk is the fat; and if the quantity of fat be deducted from the milk-solids, the "*milk-solids not fat*," which is a very constant datum, is obtained. Taking the milk-solids in country milk, and deducting the fat from it, there remains 9.65, which is the "milk-solids not fat." Similarly, the "*milk-solids not fat*" in stall-fed milk amount to 10.35 grammes per 100 c. c.

The best way of dealing with the question of watering is to assume a perfectly rigid standard of normal milk, and to treat all departures from it as sophistications. Normal country milk is of such a strength, that 100 c. c. contains 9.65 grammes of caseine, milk-sugar, and ash together—that is to say, of *milk-solids not fat*.

In one centimetre of normal milk, there is therefore $\frac{9.65}{100}$ grammes of *milk-solids not fat*.

In order to find how much genuine milk there is in 100 c. c. of a given sample of milk, the rule is, therefore, to divide the number of grammes of the *solids not fat* by 0.965.

In the next chapter the subject is still further developed.

CHAPTER IX.

THE MILK-SUPPLY OF THE LONDON WORKHOUSES.

Having had occasion to examine a large number of specimens of milk during the year 1871, I have made some observations on the subject, which, possibly, may not be deemed to be unworthy of the attention of those chemists who may have a like task before them.

The two common forms of malpractice which occur in the milk-trade are—the practice of removing the cream from the milk, and the practice of diluting the milk with water; and the testing of milk resolves itself into the detection of skimming and watering, and the measurement of the extent to which these operations have been carried.

The possibility of detecting whether or not a specimen of milk has undergone impoverishment, depends obviously on the possibility of assigning a normal composition to milk, or, at any rate, on the possibility of fixing limits beyond which the composition of milk does not vary.

From the observations of Alexander Müller and Eisenstuck, who carried out an investigation for the Royal Agricultural Society of Sweden, it appears that the milk yielded by a herd of cows remains very constant in composition throughout the year. A daily analysis of the milk given by fifteen cows, of different breeds, but uniformly well-fed, exhibited the percentage of solids in the milk as never once, during the entire year, having fallen so low as 11.5. The highest percentage of solids was 14.08. Only four times during the year did the solids fall below 12 per cent. The average was 12.8 per cent.

My own observations, made on an entirely different plan, fully bear out the statement, that cows' milk does not fall so low as 11.5 per cent. of solids, and seldom so low as 12 per cent.

The following analysis may be published:—

Date.	Desription.	Percentages.		
		Cream.	Solids dry at 100° C.	Ash.
I. 17 Feb. 1871	D. R.	10	12.24	0.76
II. 18 Feb. 1871	D. R.	....	12.04	0.68
III. 21 Feb. 1871	Cambridgeshire.	16	12.28	......
IV. " "	Surrey.	11	12.22	......
V. " "	Herts.	11	13.08	......
VI. " "	Essex.	11	11.80	......
VII. " "	Essex.	....	14.34	......
VIII. March 1871	Country milk.	9.8	12.45	0.71
IX. " "	Town-fed milk.	13.0	14.07	0.74
X. April 1871	Alderney milk.	11.5	12.65	0.70

The first two specimens, named D. R., were specimens of milk bought from milk-dealers believed to be perfectly honest. The next five specimens were samples of milk produced on farms in the different counties named in the table. Specimen VIII. is a sample taken by myself, out of some fifty or sixty gallons of milk fresh from the country. Taken altogether, the ten analyses represent the composition of an immense quantity and of a great variety of milk, and support the conclusion arrived at in Sweden by Müller and Eisenstuck.

Before leaving the subject of the normal composition of milk, it is right to refer to the laborious investigation by Goppelsröder (*vide* "Verhandlungen der Naturforschenden Gessellschaft in Basel," 1866), which, at first sight, would seem to be in opposition to the above.

In reference to Goppelsröder's paper, the remark should first be made, that that chemist does not appear to deny that the solid residue in the milk of a herd of cows keeps constantly above the level just indicated. The point which he insists upon is, that the milk of a single cow sometimes falls in richness below the normal level, and observations are cited in support of this statement. An examination of the results given in his paper does not lead me to a similar conclusion. In his paper I find many determinations of the solids in milk believed to be unsophisticated. Only four out of the entire number fall below 12 per cent. Now, it is obvious that, however constant milk may happen to be as a matter of fact, it must always be possible, by a sufficient multiplication of analyses, to exhibit an analysis showing the sample of milk as having a composition outside the normal limit of variation. In other words, there is such a thing as error of experiment, and the question to be asked respecting Goppelsröder's four isolated cases of milk, showing less than 12 per cent. of solids, is whether this divergence from the standard composition is real, or only an error of observation? Two of these instances occur in Table I., at the beginning of the paper. Among eighteen samples of milk, yielded by a single cow in eighteen consecutive days, he finds one sample yielding 10.69 per cent. of solids, and another yielding 11.41 per cent. In the same table, Goppelsröder records the percentage of cream, and the specific gravity of the milk before and after skimming. It is remarkable that the two low percentages of solids are not accompanied by low yields of cream or low specific gravities. The former of the two (viz., the 10.69 per cent. of solids) is accompanied by 10 per cent. of cream, sp. gr. 1.0316 before skimming, and sp. gr. 1.0332 after skimming; the latter (viz., the 11.41 per cent. of solids) by 11.2 per cent. of cream, sp. gr. 1.032 before and sp. gr. 1.034 after skimming. The third instance of a too low solid contents is to be met with in Table III., being the evening milk given by the last of eight cows. Percentage of solids, 11.43; cream, 7.5 per cent.; sp. gr. before skimming, 1.0315; sp. gr. after skimming, 1.0335. In this instance the cream is indeed rather low, but then the effect of skimming on the specific gravity of the milk is considerable, and the specific gravity is high.

It is perfectly true that if a little cream be removed from rich milk, and a little water (I believe it should be warm) be added to the milk, the creamometer and "lactodensimeter" may be cheated, so that there shall be want of correspondence between the indications of these instruments and the solids in the milk. But in the examples at present under discussion we are not dealing with skilfully sophisticated milk, but with milk in the natural condition as given by the cow. If the figures in the tables be correct, the cow must have, in these three instances, given milk not only abnormally poor in solids, but also in an abnormal physical condition, as if it had been manipulated by the fraudulent milk-dealer.

The fourth case of abnormally low solids occurs in Table IV., being the milk of the third cow, which is recorded as containing 9.54 per cent. of solids. In this instance, unfortunately, the yield of cream is not given. The sp. gr. before skimming was 1.0279, but the sp. gr. after skimming is not given. I observe, moreover, that the next solid contents of the table is a misprint, viz., 3.7677 instead of 13.7677 (that it is a misprint is shown by the numbers for the ash, and the number given as the ratio of the ash to the total solids).

I do not consider that Goppelsröder's four exceptional

cases are sufficiently well established; and I consider it to be a well-established fact that the milk of a herd of cows in good condition always contains more than 11.5 per cent. of solids, and that single cows almost invariably (if not always) yield milk containing more than 11.5 per cent. of solids.

In dealing with milk-supply on the large scale, we are little concerned with the possibility of single animals giving abnormal milk, and need only concern ourselves with milk of normal quality, all departures from the standard being looked upon as sophistications.

The following, which is the result of several concordant analyses of country-fed milk, may be taken as representing normal milk. In 100 grms. of milk—

Solids (dry at 100° C.) . .	12.5 grms.
Water	87.5 "
	100.0

The 12.5 grms. consist of 9.3 grms. of "solids which are not fat," and of 3.2 grms. of fat.

If we consider the changes in composition which the addition of water to milk will produce, it will be apparent that it must diminish the proportion of solids in the milk, whilst the effect of skimming is to diminish the proportion of fat, and to leave the proportion of "solids not fat" unaltered (or indeed, strictly speaking, to make a very trifling increase in the proportion of the "solids not fat").

Treating the question quite rigidly, which I believe is the proper way of dealing with it, we arrive at the following:—

Problem I.—Given the percentage of "solids not fat" ($=a$), in a specimen of sophisticated milk (*i. e.*, milk either watered or skimmed, or both),—required the number of grammes of genuine milk which was employed to form 100 grms. of it.

Answer.—Multiply the percentage of "solids not fat" by 100, and divide by 9.3. Or—

$$\frac{100}{9.3}a$$

Problem II.—Given the percentage of "solids not fat" $(= a)$, also the percentage of fat $(= b)$, in a specimen of sophisticated milk,—required the number of grammes of fat which have been removed by skimming from the genuine milk which was employed to form 100 grms. of it.

Answer.—

$$\frac{3.2}{9.3}a - b$$

In translating fat into cream, the rule is that a removal of 0.2 grm. of fat equals a removal of 1.0 grm. of cream. This rule is directly founded on experiment. I do not, however, claim a high degree of accuracy for the measurement of the cream.

Finally, a slight refinement may be noticed. If a specimen of sophisticated milk has been produced by both skimming and watering, it will be obvious, on consideration, that the extraneous water employed in manufacturing 100 grms. of it, is equal to the difference between 100 and the quantity of genuine milk employed to make 100 grms. of sophisticated milk, together with a quantity of water equal to the fat removed by skimming.

$$\text{Extraneous water} = 100 - \frac{100}{9.3}a + \frac{3.2}{9.3}a - b$$

$$= 100 - \frac{100 - 3.2}{9.3}a - b$$

An investigation of the different milks supplied to the different London Unions (which was made by me for the Government, at Mr. Rowsell's instance last year, and which is published in Mr. Rowsell's "Report on the System of Supply of Provisions for the Workhouses of the Metropolis"), will furnish an illustration of this method of interpreting the results of milk-analysis.

A sample of milk was procured from each workhouse by Mr. Rowsell at two different dates, and forwarded to me for analysis. The analysis of the earlier sample is marked I. in the following table, and that of the later sample is marked II. Samples were also forwarded to Dr. Letheby, who arrived at the same general results as myself; but either from his having slightly different specimens, or from employing different methods of analysis, his numbers sometimes exhibited some considerable departures from my own. There was, however, no difference in the practical effect of the two reports.

On inspecting the table, it will be seen the milk from twenty-eight Unions is reported upon. A well-known metropolitan Union is conspicuous by its absence, and the report would not be complete unless it were recorded that the Westminster Union refused to furnish Mr. Rowsell with information and samples.

Out of the fifty-six samples of milk only fifteen were unwatered, or nearly unwatered. Nine of these fifteen were skimmed, leaving only six that were at once unwatered and unskimmed. Accordingly about 10 per cent. of the milk supplied to London workhouses appears to be genuine. In the years 1871 and 1872, I examined about a thousand samples of milk bought in London for the *Milk Journal*, and arrived at a similar conclusion as to the general condition of the milk-trade in the metropolis (*vide* the Supplement to "Watt's Dictionary of Chemistry," article Milk-Analysis, p. 830).

It is curious to compare the language of the contract under which (as appears from Mr. Rowsell's report) the dealer supplied the various Unions with milk, with the quality of the article as exhibited by the analysis. "New unskimmed milk, unadulterated;" "Genuine as from the cow;" "Best new unskimmed milk, to produce 10 per cent. of cream," occur in the contracts.

The Fulham Union is distinguished from the rest by having a contract for "skim milk," the terms of the contract being "genuine, unadulterated milk, *pure skim*," and the Fulham Union gets an excellent quality of skimmed milk. Stepney has the most magniloquent contract, and is the worst supplied with milk.

In 100 Grammes of Sample of Milk.			Calculated.			
	Grms. of Solids not Fat.	Grms. Fat.	Grms. of Genuine Milk.	Grms. of Fat Removed.	Grms. of Cream Removed.	Grms. of Extra Water.
	$a.$	$b.$	$\frac{100}{9.3}a.$	$\frac{3.2}{9.3}a-b.$		$100-\frac{100}{9.3}a+\frac{3.2}{9.3}a-b$
Bethnal Green (St. Matthew).. I.	9.04	1.22	97.2	1.89	9.45	4.7
" " " ..II.	4.38	2.08	47.1	-0.57	-2.85	52.3
Camberwell (St. Giles)........ I.	8.37	1.14	90.0	1.74	8.70	11.7
" " ....II.	8.94	0.96	96.1	2.12	10.60	6.0
Chelsea (St. Luke) .... I.	9.36	2.24	100.6	0.98	4.90	0.4
" " ....II.	7.48	2.86	80.4	-0.28	-1.40	19.3
Fulham Union............. I.	9.09	1.52	97.8	1.61	8.05	3.8
" " ....II.	9.30	1.80	100.1	1.40	7.00	1.4
St. George's Union.......... I.	9.52	2.44	102.6	0.84	4.20	-1.8
" " ....II.	9.08	2.82	97.6	0.31	1.55	2.7
St. George-in-the-East........ I.	6.55	2.32	70.5	-0.06	-0.30	29.5
" " ....II.	5.92	1.30	63.7	0.74	3.70	37.0
St. Giles-in-the-Fields and St. George, Bloomsbury ... I.	9.13	1.50	98.2	1.65	8.25	3.4
St. Giles-in-the-Fields and St. George, Bloomsbury ...II.	7.17	1.96	77.1	0.51	2.55	23.4
Greenwich Union........... I.	6.60	2.32	71.0	-0.05	-0.25	29.0
" " ....II.	6.38	1.98	68.6	0.21	1.05	31.6
Hackney Union .... I.	9.09	3.50	97.8	-0.47	-2.35	1.7
" " II	7.40	2.54	79.6	0.00	0.00	20.4
Hampstead (St. John) .... I.	8.44	1.50	90.7	1.40	7.00	10.7
" " ....II.	7.74	3.00	83.3	-0.34	-1.70	16.4
Holborn Union............. I.	8.27	1.84	89.0	1.01	5.05	12.0
" " ....II.	7.64	2.40	82.1	0.23	1.15	18.1

Islington (St. Mary)........... I.	[illegible]	[illegible]	[illegible]	[illegible]	[illegible]	
" " ....II.	7.06	1.45	75.9	0.98	4.90	25.1
Kensington (St. Mary Abbott). I.	0 04	0.60	86.0	2.17	10.85	16.2
" " " .II.	6 08	1.26	65.4	0.83	4.15	35 4
Lambeth (St. Mary).......... I.	6.54	1.56	70 4	0.69	3.45	30.3
" " ....II.	7.08	1.22	76.1	1.22	6 10	25.1
Lewisham Union........... I.	6.42	0 96	58.3	0.90	4.50	42.6
" " ....II.	5.95	1.30	64.0	0.75	3.75	36.7
London (City of) Union....... I.	8.84	2 82	95.1	0.22	1.10	5 1
" " " ....II.	6.26	1.10	67.3	1.05	5.25	34.0
St. Marylebone............ I.	7.84	1.14	84.3	1.56	7.80	17.3
" ....II.	9.44	3.06	101.5	0.19	0.95	-1 3
Mile-end Old Town.......... I.	9.55	1.96	102.7	1.32	6.60	-1.4
" " ....II.	8.70	1.80	93.6	1.19	5.95	7.6
St. Olave's Union............ I.	7.17	1.86	77.1	0.61	3.05	23.5
" " ....II.	7.70	1.86	8[illegible].8	0 79	3.95	18.0
Paddington .... I.	7.22	1.44	77.7	1.04	5.20	23.3
" ....II.	6.06	2.16	65 2	-0.07	-0.35	34 7
St. Pancras................ I.	7.22	1.12	77.7	1.37	6 85	23.7
" ....II.	4.94	1.64	53.1	0.09	0.45	47.0
Poplar Union .... I.	7.40	0.76	79 6	1.79	8.95	22.2
" " ....II.	5.96	0 90	64.1	1.06	5.30	37.0
St. Saviour's Union .... I.	6 65	2.10	71.5	0.19	0.95	28 7
" " ....II.	6.30	1.90	67.7	0.27	1.35	32 6
Shoreditch (St. Leonard)...... I.	9.99	1.48	107 4	1.96	9.80	-5.4
" " ......II.	9 44	2.36	101 5	0.89	4.45	-0.6
Stepney .... I.	4.98	0.78	53.6	0.93	4 65	47.3
" ....II.	5.09	0 58	54.7	1.17	5.85	46.5
Strand Union .... I.	9.56	1.64	102.8	1 65	8 25	-1.2
" " ....II.	9.16	2.46	98.5	0.69	3.45	2.2
Wandsworth & Clapham Union I.	8.78	1.50	94.5	1.52	7.60	7.0
" " " II.	8.66	2.86	93.1	0.12	0 60	7.0
Whitechapel Union .... I.	5.62	0.68	60 4	0.25	1.25	39.8
" " ....II.	6.06	1.90	65.2	0.19	0.95	35.0

In Column 1 is given the designation of the sample, viz., the name of the Union which furnished it, and the number of the sample.

In Column 2 is given the number of grms. of "solids not fat" contained by 100 grms. of the sample.

In Column 3, the fat.

In Column 4, the number of grms. of genuine milk which was employed in making the 100 grms. of sample (calculated).

In Column 5, the number of grms. of fat removed by skimming from 100 grms. of sample (calculated).

In Column 6, the number of grms. of cream which had been skimmed off 100 grms. of sample (calculated).

In Column 7 is given the number of grms. of extra water which had been put into 100 grms. of sample (calculated).

Inasmuch as I have submitted the analysis of these workhouse milks to severe and elaborate treatment, it is right that some particulars should be recorded concerning the manner in which they were conducted. The ash of each milk was determined, and in no instance was it excessive in amount, showing that no mineral had been used to adulterate the milk. For organic adulteration I made no elaborate analysis; but no indication of such adulteration presented itself in the course of the examination; furthermore, I should add that I have never yet met with a case of adulteration of milk with organic substances, and believe it to be of very rare occurrence.

The solid residue dry at 100° C., was taken with great—and I believe unprecedented—accuracy. I have made a study of the taking of milk-residues, and set down the average experimental error in the solid residue as not more than 0.02 per cent. The solid residues were taken twice over, and the mean of the two closely-agreeing determinations was employed in the construction of the table.

The fats were taken with great care, but they do not pretend to so high a degree of accuracy as the total solids. It is hardly necessary to add that the numbers (designated as a) in the column headed "Grms. of Solids not Fat" were obtained by subtracting the quantity of fat ($=b$) from the quantity of total solids dry at 100° C.

The calculation of the quantities of genuine milk employed in making 100 grms. of the samples is based on the assumption, which I believe to be warranted, that milk is tolerably uniform in strength, consisting of 9.3 parts "solids not fat," 3.2 parts of fat, and 87.5 parts of water. This is the composition of country-fed milk. There is, however, an exceptionally rich milk given by highly stall-fed cows in town. This milk contains 10.0 parts of "solids not fat," 4.0 parts of fat, and 86.0 per cent of water; but it is comparatively rare.

If, in any instances in the above table, this rich stall-fed town milk has been employed instead of average country milk, then the real amount of watering and skimming in those instances is a little higher than the table exhibits. In the table there are seven examples of more than 100 grms. of genuine milk being used in making 100 grms. of the sample. Of these, one appears to be an example of this town-fed milk, the rest not being sufficiently above 100 to call for such a supposition. The example to which I refer is the Shoreditch milk, which on the first occasion yielded 9.99 per cent of "solids not fat," which is a very close approximation to the "solids not fat" in 100 parts of town-fed milk.

When a exceeds 100 a minus quantity will correspond to it in Column 7, unless the slight correction for fat obliterate the minus quantity of water. On calculating for town-fed instead of for country-fed milk, the minus-quantities in Column 7 will disappear in every instance. The calculation for town-fed milk instead of for country-fed milk, as in the table, is simple, viz., substitute 10 a for $\frac{100}{9.3}\,a$; substitute 0.4 a for $\frac{3.2}{9.3}\,a$.

The occurrence of minus-quantities in the column headed "Fat Removed" requires a word of explanation. These minus-quantities have a real and substantial meaning. They are the quantities of fat which have been the reverse of removed,—that is to say, which have been added to the milk. Whenever one of these minus-quantities occurs in the "Fat Removed" column, one of three things has happened:—Either the minus-quantity is within the limits of experimental error, as is the case with three of them (viz., –0.06, –6.05, and –0.07), or the milk was town milk, or the milk had through imperfect mixing received an undue share of the cream. There are only four cases of the kind in the table, viz., –0.57, –0.28, –0.47, and –0.34.

CHAPTER X.

CREAM.

WHEN milk is left at rest for a number of hours, it throws up a whitish layer well known as cream, which is simply milk very rich in fat.

In making examinations of cream, one of the first points which strikes the attention is the great variation in richness which it presents.

The percentages of water in different samples of cream I have found to be as follows:

Sample I.	72.20	per cent	of water.
" II.	71.20	"	"
" III.	66.36	"	"
" IV.	60.17	"	"
" V.	53.62	"	"
" VI.	50.0	"	"

And the history and complete analysis of each specimen is as follows:

SAMPLE I. Was raised by myself from an excellent specimen of country milk. It contained in 100 parts by weight—

Water	72.20
Fat	19.00
Caseine, milk-sugar, and ash . .	8.80
	100.00

SAMPLE II. Raised by myself from rich town milk. In 100 parts by weight—

Water	71.2
Fat	14.1
Caseine, &c.	14.7
	100.0

SAMPLE III. The same cream as Sample II. It had been allowed to stand for twenty-four hours longer.

In 100 parts by weight—

Water	66.36
Fat	18.87
Caseine, &c.	14.77
	100.00

SAMPLE IV. Obtained from a well-known dairy. It had been allowed to rise for only five and a quarter hours.

In 100 parts by weight—

Water	60.17
Fat	33.02
Milk-sugar, caseine, and ash . .	6.81
	100.00

SAMPLE V. From the same dairy, but had had longer time to rise.

In 100 parts by weight—

Water	53.62
Fat	38.17
Caseine, milk-sugar, and ash . .	8.21
	100.00

Sample VI. From another dairy, a very thick cream.

In 100 parts by weight—

Water	50.00
Fat	43.90
Caseine and milk-sugar . . .	5.63
Ash	0.47
	100.00

Every one of these creams is genuine and unsophisticated. It is instructive to compare the percentages of fat in the different creams.

Cream I.	19.00	fat per cent.
" II.	14.1	"
" III.	18.87	"
" IV.	33.02	"
" V.	38.17	"
" VI.	43.9	"

If we regard the determination of fat in Cream II. as questionable (for a reason to be presently explained), and if we accept the determination of fat in Cream I., to which the objection does not apply, and if we also accept the high yields of fat to which no objection can be raised, we are led to the conclusion that cream is sometimes twice as rich in fat as it is at other times. And that being granted, what becomes of the creamometer, regarded as an instrument of precision?

The rise of the cream is a physical phenomenon, depending on the difference in density between the globules of fat and the liquid in which they were floating, and also on the size of the globules. The difference between the cream and the skim-milk which has thrown it up is, that the former is milk highly charged with fat globules, and the latter is milk comparatively slightly charged with fat globules.

Cream is, in fact, a solution of caseine, milk-sugar, and milk-ash in water, holding in suspension much fat.

Skim-milk is a solution of the same ingredients which holds only little fat in suspension.

If this holds strictly true, it follows as a necessary consequence that the ratio of the water to the sum of the milk-sugar, caseine, and ash in the milk, must be preserved in the cream.

In the instance of Cream I., we have an opportunity of testing the validity of the thesis. The milk which threw up this cream had been analyzed, and found to contain water and *solids not fat* in the ratio of—

87.55 : 9.38

Cream I., as will be seen, contains water and *solids not fat* in the ratio of—

72.20 : 8.80

The theory requires that the ratio of water to *solids not fat* in the cream should be—

72.20 : 8.31

The correspondence is sufficiently near to show that the theory holds in this instance.

The case of Creams II. and III. we will deal with presently. Passing on to Cream IV., we have ratio of water to *solids not fat*—

60.17 : 6.81

Theory requires

60.17 : 6.43

In Cream V., the ratio is—

53.62 : 8.21)

and it should be

53.62 : 5.63

which does not agree very well.

In Cream VI., the ratio is—

50.0 : 6.1

It should be

50.0 : 5.36

which is a sufficiently close approximation.

In Creams II. and III., which were drawn off the same sample of milk (which, by the way, was the rich town-fed milk), and which differ by being drawn after different periods had elapsed, we have—

In Cream II., the ratio is—

71.2 : 14.7

In Cream III.—

66.36 : 14.77

the ratio required by the theory being

85.93 : 10.07

It would therefore appear that the rich town-fed milk is apt to throw up a little caseine along with the fat. In general, however, the cream consists simply of fat *plus* a solution of caseine, milk-sugar, and ash, of just the same strength as existed in the milk which gave the cream. The exception in favor of the cream given by town-fed milk must even be received with extreme caution by reason of the great difficulty of the cream analysis, and the certainty that the whole experimental error falls on the determination of *solids not fat*, and that any imperfection in the analysis tends to enlarge the *solids not fat.*

There is far more difficulty in drying a cream-residue than in drying a milk-residue: there is also the chance of loss of fat, and any imperfections of this kind would make *solids not fat* too high.

In this place it is proper to say that the analysis of cream is very like the analysis of milk; only that much less than five grammes should be taken for the determination of water. The cream must be weighed out—not measured. About two grammes is ample for the determination of water. The drying must be made in the water-bath, and may take as long as six or eight hours. The question is often put—Has a given specimen of cream been thickened with gum or such like material?

A very decided answer may be given in the negative if the ratio of water to *solids not fat* is that required by the solution of caseine, milk-sugar, and ash, constituting the non-fatty portion of milk.

Should there be too much *solids not fat*, then the inquiry must be made whether the excess be caseine.

Cream is sometimes suspected of being stiffened with starch; this, of course, is at once detected by testing with a little iodine, which will at once strike a blue, if any such adulteration had been practised.

CHAPTER XI.

BUTTER.

In the thickest varieties of cream there is probably incipient cohesion of the fat globules. In butter the fat has actually cohered; and it ought also to have been washed and very slightly salted. Butter is milk-fat, not indeed in a state of absolute chemical purity, but with a certain comparatively small proportion of water, and a little salt.

The first point to be inquired into is, how much water may butter contain? In fresh Devonshire butter I found—

Fat, ...	82.7
Salt, ...	1.1
Water, and trace of organic matter .	16.2
	100.0

In Normandy butter—

Fat, ...	82.1
Salt, ...	1.8
Water, and trace of organic matter .	16.1
	100.0

These results agree with Mr. Way's observations; and commercial fresh butter may, accordingly, contain some 18 per cent. of water, including the touch of salt. Salt butter may apparently contain some 6 per cent. of salt. The analysis of butter is made as follows:—

First, great care must be taken to get a fair sample of the

lot. This is, perhaps, best done by taking two specimens, one from the edge of the butter, and another from the centre. About one gramme of butter is enough for the estimation of water. This is to be weighed into one of the little platinum dishes, and dried in the bath as if it were a milk-residue. After three hours' drying it should be weighed, and returned to the bath, and weighed at intervals of an hour till constant. The drying up of butter is tedious, like the drying up of cream. Having dried it up, the residue is to be dissolved in dry ether, filtered, and the ethereal solution evaporated to dryness, and the residue dried in the water-bath. This second drying is a very easy one.

The mineral matter is estimated by burning off the fat and weighing the residue.

The "organic matter not fat" may be estimated by difference. It may also be estimated directly. For this purpose several grammes of butter are weighed out, and dried for a short time in a platinum dish in the water-bath, and then subjected to the action of dry ether, which will dissolve out the fat and leave the rest. The ethereal solution is to be decanted off, and the residue dried up in the water-bath, weighed, and ignited, and again weighed. The difference between the two weights is the weight of the organic matter not fat.

With regard to the question of admixture of foreign fats with milk-fat, we are unable, in the present condition of our knowledge, to deal with that part of the problem.

As has been said, milk-fat is a mixture of the ethers of glycerine, which constitute the common fats. It contains, it is true, a trace of butyrine, in addition to the commoner glycerides; and it is possible that, by an extraction of the butyric acid, we might arrive at data of some value in forming a judgment of the quality of the fat. But investigation is required before that could be depended upon; and at present the chemist will act wisely in declining to pronounce on the difference between butter-fat and other fat.

In the butter-trade there are certainly two kinds of fraud which are very rife. The one is the passing off of butter of inferior flavor for butter of high flavor. The other is the making of butter take up too much water and salt.

An investigation, which I had the honor of making for Government, illustrates how these two descriptions of fraud are practised in the London workhouses.

I quote the report *in extenso*:—

"REPORT ON THE BUTTER SUPPLIED TO THE METROPOLITAN UNIONS.

"Good butter, as it occurs in the market, consists of 12.5 per cent. of water, 1.0 per cent. of salt, a little caseine, and the rest of butter-fats; salt butter may contain 5 per cent. of salt.

"The falsifications to which butter is liable are said to be the adulteration of it with organic substances like starch or gelatine, substances which are not fat; adulteration with fat which is not butter-fat; undue moisture, and saltness.

"In the fifty specimens of workhouse butter sent to me by Mr. F. W. Rowsell between 8th May and 7th July, 1871, I have not noted any case of adulteration with starch or other organic matter which is not fat.

"The adulteration of butter-fat with foreign fats—that is to say, with fat which is not the fat of butter—is not capable of being ascertained with precision in the present state of chemical methods of analysis.

"In the instance of butter No. 6, viz., 'St. Giles-in-the-Fields (officers),' I have met with a butter in which there appears to be some foreign fat.

"The point brought out by my examination is the extraordinary way in which many of the butters have been made to take up water.

"I have also given an opinion on the quality of the butter, or its flavor. This opinion was obtained from professed butter-dealers.

"Fourteen of the butters contain an undue proportion of water, viz., Kensington, Marylebone, St. Luke's (Chelsea), Paddington (fresh), Paddington (paupers), Whitechapel (inmates), City of London (inmates), Holborn (inmates), Camberwell, Stepney (inmates), Clapham and Wandsworth (inmates), Hackney (inmates), St. George's-in-the-East (inmates), Greenwich (inmates).

"The worst case of undue wetness and saltness is 'Whitechapel, inmates,' which contains 35.6 per cent. of salt and water; and, after deducting the small quantity of organic matter which is not fat, is seen to contain only some 60 per cent. of fat.

No.	Name.	Water.	Salt.	
1	St. George's (Kensington Workhouse).	8.6	4.5	Rank.
2	Kensington (salt)...................	23.7	6.0	Wretched.
3	Marylebone.........................	18.2	6 9	Tolerable.
4	Westminster (information refused)....	....	....	
5	St. Luke's, Chelsea..................	14.5	3.2	Fair.
6	St. Giles-in-the-Fields (officers)	13.2	0.7	Very rank.
7	St. Giles-in-the-Fields (paupers)	12.5	1.0	Bad.
8	Strand..............................	9.7	2.7	Tolerably good.
9	Fulham (officers)....................	12.9	0.1	Very good.
10	Fulham	13.1	4.3	Good.
11	Paddington (fresh)	23.6	1.0	Rather rank.
12	Paddington (paupers)................	16.5	4.9	Bad.
13	Whitechapel (officers)	12.4	1.0	Middling.
14	Whitechapel (inmates)..............	24.9	10.7	Very bad.
15	Mile-end Old Town (officers)..........	11.6	2.1	Good.
16	Mile-end Old Town (inmates).........	11.5	1.2	Very fair.
17	City of London Mile-end Workhouse (officers).................	13.7	1.1	Good.
18	City of London Mile-end Workhouse (inmates)	20.0	2.6	Bad.
19	Shoreditch (officers)	13.2	1.0	Good.
20	Shoreditch (inmates)................	15.3	4.7	Bad.
21	Bethnell Green (officers).............	11.7	....	Good.
22	Bethnell Green (inmates)	11.3	2.4	Middling.
23	St. Pancras (officers).................	12.8	1.0	Bad.
24	St. Pancras (inmates)................	12.2	5.1	Very bad.
25	Holborn (officers)....................	8.2	2.8	Good.
26	Holborn (inmates)...................	19.7	7.0	Middling.
27	Lambeth (officers)...................	13.3	1.5	Bad.
28	Lambeth (inmates)..................	13.2	2.1	Exceedingly bad.
29	Camberwell.........	14.7	8.1	Exceedingly bad.
30	Islington	9.8	4.4	Tolerable.
31	Poplar (officers)	12.0	0.9	Middling.
32	Poplar (inmates)	12.9	6.3	Very bad.
33	Stepney (officers)....................	12.7	....	Middling.
34	Stepney (inmates)..................	16.5	0.7	Nasty.
35	St. Olaves (officers)..................	11.3	2.3	Pretty Good.
36	St. Olaves (inmates).................	14.3	3.5	Fair.
37	Hampstead (officers)................	11.6	0.1	Good.
38	Hampstead (inmates)	12.2	0.4	Fair.
39	Wandsworth and Clapham (officers)...	13.3	1.7	Very good.
40	Wandsworth and Clapham (inmates)..	15.3	7.3	Bad.
41	St. Saviour's (officers)	11.9	0 5	Very bad.
42	St. Saviour's (inmates)...............	12.6	4.4	Fair.
43	Hackney (officers)..................	14.2	1.1	Good.
44	Hackney (inmates)	16.6	4.7	Tolerable.
45	St. George's-in-the-East (officers)	9.9	3.5	Good.
46	St. George's-in-the-East (inmates).....	15.4	5.6	Bad.
47	Greenwich (officers)..................	10.9	1.7	Good.
48	Greenwich (inmates).................	19.4	5.9	Fair.
49	Lewisham (officers)..................	12.1	0.4	Tolerable.
50	Lewisham (inmates).................	10.7	5.4	Good.

J. Alfred Wanklyn.

London, *July* 11*th*, 1871."

CHAPTER XII.

CHEESE.

Cheese consists mainly of caseine, milk-fat, a little salt and phosphate of lime, and water. It is, as is well known, prepared by subjecting milk to the action of rennet, which coagulates it, and then pressing the curds, which, after treatment, constitute the cheese. There is great variation in the composition of cheese.

According to Payen, the water ranges from 30 to 62 per cent.; the fat, according to the same chemist, appears to vary from about 20 to about 30 per cent. The percentage of caseine appears to range from 15 to 35, and the mineral matter from $4\frac{1}{4}$ to 7.

The analysis of cheese is managed as follows:—The water is determined by taking about one gramme, and drying it in the water-bath in a small platinum dish (one of the little dishes used for milk-residues will answer very well), until it ceases to lose in weight. After the determination of the water, the residue may be ignited, and the ash weighed.

For the determination of fat and caseine, it is well to take a larger quantity of cheese. About ten grammes is a convenient quantity. The cheese should be weighed out, having been first cut up into small pieces, and then introduced into a small flask. It is then boiled with dry ether, and the resulting ethereal solution of the fat is decanted off; the boiling and decantation is repeated twice, and, finally, the ethereal solutions are carefully evaporated down in a platinum dish, and the fat which is left behind is dried at 100° C. and weighed.

In the above operation, great care must be taken to exhaust thoroughly with ether; the mass may be got out of the flask and powdered up in a mortar if necessary. It is also well to moisten with a few drops of strong alcohol before adding the ether. Having, as aforesaid, obtained from the cheese an ethereal solution of the fat, and having disposed of this ethereal solution, we return to the mass which refuses to dissolve in the ether. This consists of caseine, possibly of milk-sugar as well, and certainly of salt and phosphate of lime. It is to be treated first with strong alcohol, and then washed with boiling water, and then dried in a platinum dish. The dry residue (which consists of caseine and phosphate of lime or ash) is then weighed, ignited, and weighed again: the difference, *i. e.*, the loss on ignition, is the caseine.

In order to determine the milk-sugar, the alcoholic and aqueous solutions are to be evaporated to dryness, the residue weighed and ignited, and the loss on ignition will include the sugar.

In analysis of cheese it is necessary that a caution should be given respecting the large amount of ash in cheese. As much as 7 per cent. of ash may be present in cheese, without adulteration with mineral matter having been practised.

It has been stated that oxide of lead has been found in cheese. Should any such case arise, it is very easily dealt with. The cheese-ash (which, in such a case, should be got in a porcelain crucible, since lead attacks platinum) is tested for lead by means of sulphuretted hydrogen.

CHAPTER XIII.

KOUMISS.

In addition to cream, butter, and cheese, the derivatives of milk include whey and butter-milk, which latter do not call for any special notice. There is, however, another derivative of milk, which ought not to be passed over. Milk can be got to ferment and yield a sort of milk-wine, which goes by the name of koumiss. In Tartary, where mare's milk is used for the purpose, the drink which results is of great importance as an article of nourishment for the population. The use of koumiss is said, moreover, to impart immunity from phthisis, and an attempt is being made in this country to produce an English koumiss for the use of patients whose nutrition is impaired. It is hoped that koumiss will prove to be at least as efficacious as cod-liver-oil is believed by many people to be.

The following analyses of koumiss manufactured in London by E. Chapman & Co. were made in my laboratory.

It should be mentioned, that inasmuch as mare's milk contains a larger proportion of sugar than cow's milk, an addition of a little sugar is made to the milk before it is set to ferment.

In "full koumiss," forty-eight hours old, which had a specific gravity of 1.032 at 67° Fah., I found—

In 100 parts by weight—

Water	87.32
Alcohol	1.00
Carbonic acid	0.90
Solids	10.78
	100.00

The 10.78 parts of solids contained—

Caseine	2.84
Lactose and lactic acid	6.60
Fat	0.68
Ash	0.66
	10.78

Some of the same sample of koumiss, after having been kept for six days at 62° Fah., contained in 100 parts by weight—

Water	88.47
Alcohol	1.60
Carbonic acid	1.50
Solids	8.43
	100.00

A determination of the proportion of lactic acid in this koumiss, on its tenth day, or eight days older than when first examined, showed 1.1 per cent. When thirty-five days old this koumiss had a specific gravity of 1.023, and contained in 100 parts by weight—

Water	89.16
Alcohol	1.80
Carbonic acid	1.50
Solids	7.54
	100.00

The solids consisting of—

Caseine	2.57
Lactose and lactic acid	3.82
Fat	.50
Ash	.65
	7.54

To begin with, koumiss contains about the same percentage of solids as skimmed milk; but, as will be observed on inspecting these analyses, and, as might have been expected, koumiss, as it grows older, loses sugar and total solids.

It is claimed for koumiss that it presents the caseine in a form specially assimilable by invalids, and that koumiss will sometimes nourish persons when nothing else will nourish. It is not the place, in a work like the present, to discuss how far these claims are made good, but it is right to call attention to the fact of such claims having been put forward.

CHAPTER XIV.

CONDENSED AND PRESERVED MILK.

This preparation of milk, which is now much in vogue, consists of milk which has been evaporated down *in vacuo.*

When it is intended to keep for any lengthened period, it is mixed with a considerable proportion of pure cane-sugar.

When it is not required to keep for longer than two or three days, it is simply tinned, and not mixed with sugar.

The condensed milk is strictly what its name signifies; for, on being mixed with the appropriate quantity of water, it regenerates milk. The preserved milk, too, regenerates milk on being diluted; only it is sweet, owing to the sugar employed in the preservation.

A year ago, a report was spread that these preserved milks were preserved skim-milk, and not preserved new milk. This report, which was spread by a Government official who ought to have known better, is a most undeserved calumny.

I have myself examined the principal brands of preserved and condensed milk which are in the London market, and find that the milk which had been condensed, or condensed and preserved, had been charged with its due proportion of fat.

In the Anglo-Swiss, I found 9.9 per cent. of fat. In the product of the English Condensed Milk Company (Limited), I found 10.4 per cent. of fat in the preserved milk and 12.11 per cent. in the condensed milk.

The method of analyzing condensed or preserved milk is that recommended for cheese. Great care must be taken in the estimation of the fat. Disintegration with alcohol, or actual pulverization in a mortar, is to be recommended, in order to bring the ether completely into relation with the mass. The following analyses of the produce of the English Condensed Milk Company may be of interest :—

PRESERVED MILK.

In 100 parts by weight—

Water	20.5
Fat	10.4
Caseine	11.0
Ash	2.0
Cane and milk-sugar	56.1
	100.00

CONDENSED MILK.

Water	51.12
Fat	12.11
Caseine	13.64
Milk-sugar	20.36
Ash	2.77
	100.00

CHAPTER XV.

POISONOUS MILK AND MILK-PANICS.

It is known that violent mental emotion exercises an unfavorable influence on the secretion of the mammary gland; and a fit of anger has rendered the milk of the human mother poisonous to the child. No doubt the milk of the cow is more or less liable to similar influences; and cows which are giving milk should not be driven or harassed in any way. Diet, too, has an effect on the quality of the milk; a purgative administered to the mother often taking effect on the child. Poisonous herbs fed on by the cow contaminate the milk; and a very well-known example in point is afforded by turnipy butter, which derives its very objectionable (though not poisonous) properties from turnips on which the cow has happened to feed. All this tends to show the importance of attending to the health of milk-giving cows, and to the kind of fodder on which they are fed.

Milk, after it has been yielded by the animal, may suffer contamination at a later stage. A case is recorded where, in the process of milking, which was performed by persons recovering from scarlet fever, the infection of scarlet fever was conveyed by the milk to children who drank it. This is, I believe, authentic enough.

In addition to these genuine instances of milk-poisoning, a very subtle kind of poisoning has been described. It has been said that, if a very minute qantity of water from a foul well be mixed with a very large quantity of milk, the whole mass of milk will become poisonous. And, as is well known, considerable alarm has been created in the west-end of London, by a report that the milk purveyed by a certain milk-company had occasioned an outbreak of typhoid fever in Marylebone, and the parishes adjacent to Marylebone.

It is, however, important to record that the result of investigation has been to demonstrate the groundlessness of these alarms. The returns of the Registrar-General, which are now before the public, show that Marylebone has seldom been so free from typhoid fever as during the period of the supposed epidemic.

The history of this supposed epidemic of typhoid fever, or, as it would be more correctly designated, the history of the milk-panic of 1873, is very instructive in many ways.

Early in August, 1873, several children of an eminent west-end physician were ill of typhoid fever, and their father attributed the disease to the milk which they took. The doctor's family was supplied with milk by the Dairy Reform Company. On communicating his suspicions to neighboring medical men, and to the medical officer of health for the district, a number of cases of alleged typhoid were found among customers of the same dairy, a strangely large proportion of these cases occurring in the families of medical men. It was said that, naturally enough, the superior knowledge of medical men was the explanation of the apparent preference of the disease for their families, and that by and by the anomaly would disappear when the multitudes of unrecognized cases in non-medical families became sufficiently serious to force recognition of their real nature. The physician and the medical officer of health (in a most public-spirited manner, as it was called) addressed a peremptory order to the directors of the milk-company to stop selling milk; the fears of the physician even reached the local Government Board, and an official investigation was ordered.

Meanwhile the press took up the subject, and the medical

papers and the non-technical newspapers vied with one another in sensational descriptions of the "Outbreak of Typhoid Fever," its source, and the wickedness or recklessness of the milk-company which had caused it.

At the outset of the panic, the leading journal published a list of twenty-three households wherein inmates were said to have been poisoned by the Dairy Reform Company. With the assistance of my friend Mr. Cooper, I took the trouble to inquire into some of these cases. In one of these households there was no one ill, and there had been no one ill. In another household, there had been only a little summer diarrhœa. In a third, the lady had been taken ill in Munich, where typhoid fever is known to be rife. In a fourth, where the servants were affected, the water in the kitchen was bad, the general supply to the house being good. The servant had, moreover, been a day's journey into the country during the very hot weather, and had been overheated. I did not pursue the investigation further.

The official report on the condition of the farms whence the milk-company derive their supply of milk, has not yet been published. A gentleman who attended on behalf of the Dairy Reform Company, has, however, written to *The Times* newspaper a letter purporting to give an outline of the conclusions arrived at by the commission. From this letter we gather that at the time of the inquiry there were no cases of typhoid on any of the farms, and that there had been no recent cases. Instead, however, of calling public attention to that most satisfactory result of the inquiry, the writer of the letter dwelt upon a very doubtful case which had occurred on one of the farms at a rather remote period. The supposed epidemic was alleged to be at its height about the 10th of August, and before the beginning of August nothing had been heard of any epidemic. On the supposition of infection from one of the farms, we should hardly look for the case before the beginning of July. The case, however, to which the writer of the letter directed attention, dated as far back as before the 8th of June. The case in question was that of the farmer who had occupied one of the farms, and who died on the 8th of June. Even the nature of his illness is involved in doubt. The man's death, indeed, is entered on the register as caused by heart disease, from which he had been known to have suffered for at least a year; and the suddenness of his death is quite in accordance with the register. Some few weeks before his death he had an attack of diarrhœa of a suspicious character, and that circumstance was seized upon as a reason for setting down his case as one of typhoid fever. It is, however, hard to believe that the excreta from this man can have poisoned the farm-well, and that the water from that well should have poisoned the milk which was sent to London, without poisoning any one on the farm; and the wonder becomes the greater since the water from the well was occasionally, though not usually, employed for domestic purposes.

As already mentioned, the reported case of typhoid occurred very much too early to account for what was called the London outbreak. It is very curious to observe that the termination of the outbreak did not accord with the theory. That which was designated the "infected milk," ceased to be supplied to London on the 11th of August, and forthwith—within two or three days—the epidemic was reported to have declined. The period of incubation in typhoid fever is ten days or thereabouts, therefore the stoppage of the poisoning on the 11th should not have been felt till towards the 21st.

It has been mentioned that when the returns of the Registrar-General were published, the mortality in Marylebone from typhoid fever was found to have been lower than usual. The following are the returns, week by week, embracing the whole period of the panic. Population of Marylebone, 159,254.

The deaths from typhoid fever in Marylebone were as follows:—

During week ending	5th July	0
"	12th "	1
"	19th "	2
"	26th "	0
"	2d August . . .	1
"	9th " . . .	1
"	16th " . . .	3
"	23d " . . .	2
"	30th " . . .	2
"	6th September . . .	2
	Total during the ten weeks	14

Being at the rate of rather less than one per 100,000 per week.

A poison which does not poison you if you take it in aqueous solution, but poisons a whole township when that same aqueous solution is diluted with milk a hundred or a thousand fold, and whose period of incubation is sometimes two months and sometimes three days, according to the exigencies of your case, must be singular indeed. And when such a poison seems to have ravaged a whole parish, it marks its ravages most appropriately by a diminution in the death-rate.

THE END.

Weisbach's Mechanics.

New and Revised Edition.

8vo. Cloth. $10.00.

A MANUAL OF THE MECHANICS OF ENGINEERING, and of the Construction of Machines. By JULIUS WEISBACH, PH. D. Translated from the fourth augmented and improved German edition, by ECKLEY B. COXE, A.M., Mining Engineer. Vol. I.—Theoretical Mechanics. 1,100 pages, and 902 wood-cut illustrations.

ABSTRACT OF CONTENTS.—Introduction to the Calculus—The General Principles of Mechanics—Phoronomics, or the Purely Mathematical Theory of Motion—Mechanics, or the General Physical Theory of Motion – Statics of Rigid Bodies—The Application of Statics to Elasticity and Strength—Dynamics of Rigid Bodies – Statics of Fluids - Dynamics of Fluids—The Theory of Oscillation, etc.

"The present edition is an entirely new work, greatly extended and very much improved. It forms a text-book which must find its way into the hands, not only of every student, but of every engineer who desires to refresh his memory or acquire clear ideas on doubtful points."—*Manufacturer and Builder.*

"We hope the day is not far distant when a thorough course of study and education as such shall be demanded of the practising engineer, and with this view we are glad to welcome this translation to our tongue and shores of one of the most able of the educators of Europe."—*The Technologist.*

Francis' Lowell Hydraulics.

Third Edition.

4to. Cloth. $15.00.

LOWELL HYDRAULIC EXPERIMENTS — being a Selec tion from Experiments on Hydraulic Motors, on the Flow o Water over Weirs, and in Open Canals of Uniform Rectangula Section, made at Lowell, Mass. By J. B. FRANCIS, Civil Engineer Third edition, revised and enlarged, including many New Ex periments on Gauging Water in Open Canals, and on the Flow through Submerged Orifices and Diverging Tubes. With 2 copperplates, beautifully engraved, and about 100 new pages o text.

The work is divided into parts. PART I., on hydraulic motors, include ninety-two experiments on an improved Fourneyron Turbine Water-Wheel of about two hundred horse-power, with rules and tables for the constructio of similar motors; thirteen experiments on a model of a centre-vent water wheel of the most simple design, and thirty-nine experiments on a centre-ven water-wheel of about two hundred and thirty horse-power.

PART II. includes seventy-four experiments made for the purpose of deter mining the form of the formula for computing the flow of water over weirs nine experiments on the effect of back-water on the flow over weirs; eighty eight experiments made for the purpose of determining the formula for com puting the flow over weirs of regular or standard forms, with several table of comparisons of the new formula with the results obtained by former experi menters; five experiments on the flow over a dam in which the crest was of th same form as that built by the Essex Company across the Merrimack River a Lawrence, Massachusetts; twenty-one experiments on the effect of observin the depths of water on a weir at different distances from the weir; an exten sive series of experiments made for the purpose of determining rules fo gauging streams of water in open canals, with tables for facilitating the same and one hundred and one experiments on the discharge of water through sub merged orifices and diverging tubes, the whole being fully illustrated b twenty-three double plates engraved on copper.

In 1855 the proprietors of the Locks and Canals on Merrimack River con sented to the publication of the first edition of this work, which contained selection of the most important hydraulic experiments made at Lowell up t that time. In this edition the principal hydraulic experiments made there subsequent to 1855, have been added, including the important series abov mentioned, for determining rules for the gauging the flow of water in ope canals, and the interesting series on the flow through a submerged Venturi' tube, in which a larger flow was obtained than any we find recorded.

Francis on Cast-Iron Pillars.

8vo. Cloth. $2.00.

ON THE STRENGTH OF CAST-IRON PILLARS, with Tables for the use of Engineers, Architects, and Builders. By JAMES B. FRANCIS, Civil Engineer.

Merrill's Iron Truss Bridges.

Second Edition.

4to. Cloth. $5.00.

IRON TRUSS BRIDGES FOR RAILROADS. The Method of Calculating Strains in Trusses, with a careful comparison of the most prominent Trusses, in reference to economy in combination, etc., etc. By Brevet Colonel WILLIAM E. MERRILL, U.S.A., Major Corps of Engineers. Nine lithographed plates of illustrations.

"The work before us is an attempt to give a basis for sound reform in this feature of railroad engineering, by throwing 'additional light upon the method of calculating the maxima strains that can come upon any part of a bridge truss, and upon the manner of proportioning each part, so that it shall be as strong relatively to its own strains as any other part, and so that the entire bridge may be strong enough to sustain several times as great strains as the greatest that can come upon it in actual use.' "—*Scientific American.*

"The author has presented his views in a clear and intelligent manner, and the ingenuity displayed in coloring the figures so as to present certain facts to the eye forms no inappreciable part of the merits of the work. The reduction of the 'formulæ for obtaining the strength, volume, and weight of a cast-iron pillar under a strain of compression,' will be very acceptable to those who have occasion hereafter to make investigations involving these conditions. As a whole, the work has been well done."—*Railroad Gazette, Chicago.*

Humber's Strains in Girders.

18mo. Cloth. $2.50.

A HANDY BOOK FOR THE CALCULATION OF STRAINS IN GIRDERS and Similar Structures, and their Strength, consisting of Formulæ and Corresponding Diagrams, with numerous details for practical application. By WILLIAM HUMBER. Fully illustrated.

Shreve on Bridges and Roofs.

8vo, 87 wood-cut illustrations. Cloth. $5.00.

A TREATISE ON THE STRENGTH OF BRIDGES AND ROOFS—comprising the determination of Algebraic formulas for Strains in Horizontal, Inclined or Rafter, Triangular, Bowstring, Lenticular and other Trusses, from fixed and moving loads, with practical applications and examples, for the use of Students and Engineers. By SAMUEL H. SHREVE, A.M., Civil Engineer.

The rules for the determination of strains given in this work, in the shape of formulas, are deduced from a few well-known mechanical laws, and are not based upon assumed conditions; the processes are given and applications made of the results, so that it is equally valuable as a text-book for the Student and as a manual for the Practical Engineer. Among the examples are the Greithausen Bridge, the Kuilemberg Bridge, a bridge of the Saltash type, and many other compound trusses, whose strains are calculated by methods which are not only free from the use of the higher mathematics, but are as simple and accurate, and as readily applied, as those which are used in proportioning a Warren Girder or other simple truss.

The Kansas City Bridge.

4to. Cloth. $6.00

WITH AN ACCOUNT OF THE REGIMEN OF THE MISSOURI RIVER, and a description of the Methods used for Founding in that River. By O. CHANUTE, Chief Engineer, and GEORGE MORISON, Assistant Engineer. Illustrated with five lithographic views and twelve plates of plans.

Illustrations.

VIEWS.—View of the Kansas City Bridge, August 2, 1869. Lowering Caisson No. 1 into position. Caisson for Pier No. 4 brought into position. View of Foundation Works, Pier No. 4. Pier No. 1.

PLATES.—I. Map showing location of Bridge. II. Water Record—Cross Section of River—Profile of Crossing—Pontoon Protection. III. Water Deadener—Caisson No. 2—Foundation Works, Pier No. 3. IV. Foundation Works, Pier No. 4. V. Foundation Works, Pier No. 4. VI. Caisson No. 5—Sheet Piling at Pier No. 6—Details of Dredges—Pile Shoe—Beton Box. VII. Masonry—Draw Protection—False Works between Piers 3 and 4. VIII. Floating Derricks. IX. General Elevation—176 feet span. X. 248 feet span. XI. Plans of Draw. XII. Strain Diagrams.

Clarke's Quincy Bridge.

4to. Cloth. $7.50.

DESCRIPTION OF THE IRON RAILWAY Bridge across the Mississippi River at Quincy, Illinois. By THOMAS CURTIS CLARKE, Chief Engineer. Illustrated with twenty-one lithographed plans.

Illustrations.

PLATES.—General Plan of Mississippi River at Quincy, showing location of Bridge. II*a*. General Sections of Mississippi River at Quincy, showing location of Bridge. II*b*. General Sections of Mississippi River at Quincy, showing location of Bridge. III. General Sections of Mississippi River at Quincy, showing location of Bridge. IV. Plans of Masonry. V. Diagram of Spans, showing the Dimensions, Arrangement of Panels, etc. VI. Two hundred and fifty feet span, and details. VII. Three hundred and sixty feet Pivot Draw. VIII. Details of three hundred and sixty feet Draw. IX. Ice-Breakers, Foundations of Piers and Abutments, Water Table, and Curve of Deflections. X. Foundations of Pier 2, in Process of Construction. XI. Foundations of Pier 3, and its Protection. XII. Foundations of Pier 3, in Process of Construction, and Steam Dredge. XIII. Foundations of Piers 5 to 18, in Process of Construction. XIV. False Works, showing Process of Handling and Setting Stone. XV. False Works for Raising Iron Work of Superstructure. XVI. Steam Dredge used in Foundations 9 to 18. XVII. Single Bucket Dredge used in Foundations of Bay Piers. XVIII. Saws used for Cutting Piles under water. XIX. Sand Pump and Concrete Box. XX Masonry Travelling Crane.

Whipple on Bridge Building.

8vo, Illustrated. Cloth. $4.00.

AN ELEMENTARY AND PRACTICAL TREATISE ON BRIDGE BUILDING. An enlarged and improved edition of the Author's original work. By S. WHIPPLE, C. E., Inventor of the Whipple Bridges, &c. Second Edition.

The design has been to develop from Fundamental Principles a system easy of comprehension, and such as to enable the attentive reader and student to judge understandingly for himself, as to the relative merits of different plans and combinations, and to adopt for use such as may be most suitable for the cases he may have to deal with.

It is hoped the work may prove an appropriate Text-Book upon the subject treated of, for the Engineering Student, and a useful manual for the Practicing Engineer and Bridge Builder.

Stoney on Strains.

New and Revised Edition, with numerous illustrations.

Royal 8vo, 664 pp. Cloth. $15.00.

THE THEORY OF STRAINS IN GIRDERS and Similar Structures, with Observations on the Application of Theory to Practice, and Tables of Strength and other Properties of Materials. By BINDON B. STONEY, B. A.

Roebling's Bridges.

Imperial folio. Cloth. $25.00.

LONG AND SHORT SPAN RAILWAY BRIDGES. By JOHN A. ROEBLING, C. E. Illustrated with large copperplate engravings of plans and views.

List of Plates

1. Parabolic Truss Railway Bridge. 2, 3, 4, 5, 6. Details of Parabolic Truss, with centre span 500 feet in the clear. 7. Plan and View of a Bridge over the Mississippi River, at St. Louis, for railway and common travel. 8, 9, 10, 11, 12. Details and View of St. Louis Bridge. 13. Railroad Bridge over the Ohio.

Diedrichs' Theory of Strains.

8vo. Cloth. $5.00.

A Compendium for the Calculation and Construction of Bridges, Roofs, and Cranes, with the Application of Trigonometrical Notes. Containing the most comprehensive information in regard to the Resulting Strains for a permanent Load, as also for a combined (Permanent and Rolling) Load. In two sections adapted to the requirements of the present time. By JOHN DIEDRICHS. Illustrated by numerous plates and diagrams.

"The want of a compact, universal and popular treatise on the Construction of Roofs and Bridges—especially one treating of the influence of a variable load—and the unsatisfactory essays of different authors on the subject, induced me to prepare this work."

Whilden's Strength of Materials.

12mo. Cloth. $2.00.

ON THE STRENGTH OF MATERIALS used in Engineering Construction. By J. K. Whilden.

Campin on Iron Roofs.

Large 8vo. Cloth. $2.00.

ON THE CONSTRUCTION OF IRON ROOFS. A Theoretical and Practical Treatise. By Francis Campin. With wood-cuts and plates of Roofs lately executed.

"The mathematical formulas are of an elementary kind, and the process admits of an easy extension so as to embrace the prominent varieties of iron truss bridges. The treatise, though of a practical scientific character, may be easily mastered by any one familiar with elementary mechanics and plane trigonometry."

Holley's Railway Practice.

1 vol. folio. Cloth. $12.00.

AMERICAN AND EUROPEAN RAILWAY PRACTICE, in the Economical Generation of Steam, including the materials and construction of Coal-burning Boilers, Combustion, the Variable Blast, Vaporization, Circulation, Super-heating, Supplying and Heating Feed-water, &c., and the adaptation of Wood and Coke-burning Engines to Coal-burning; and in Permanent Way, including Road-bed, Sleepers, Rails, Joint Fastenings, Street Railways, &c., &c. By Alexander L. Holley, B. P. With 77 lithographed plates.

"This is an elaborate treatise by one of our ablest civil engineers, on the construction and use of locomotives, with a few chapters on the building of Railroads. * * * All these subjects are treated by the author, who is a first-class railroad engineer, in both an intelligent and intelligible manner. The facts and ideas are well arranged, and presented in a clear and simple style, accompanied by beautiful engravings, and we presume the work will be regarded as indispensable by all who are interested in a knowledge of the construction of railroads and rolling stock, or the working of locomotives."—*Scientific American.*

Henrici's Skeleton Structures.

8vo. Cloth. $1.50.

SKELETON STRUCTURES, especially in their Application to the building of Steel and Iron Bridges. By OLAUS HENRICI. With folding plates and diagrams.

By presenting these general examinations on Skeleton Structures, with particular application for Suspended Bridges, to Engineers, I venture to express the hope that they will receive these theoretical results with some confidence, even although an opportunity is wanting to compare them with practical results. O. H.

Useful Information for Railway Men.

Pocket form. Morocco, gilt, $2.00.

Compiled by W. G. HAMILTON, Engineer. Fifth edition, revised and enlarged. 570 pages.

"It embodies many valuable formulæ and recipes useful for railway men, and, indeed, for almost every class of persons in the world. The 'information' comprises some valuable formulæ and rules for the construction of boilers and engines, masonry, properties of steel and iron, and the strength of materials generally."—*Railroad Gazette, Chicago.*

Brooklyn Water Works.

1 vol. folio. Cloth. $25.00.

A DESCRIPTIVE ACCOUNT OF THE CONSTRUCTION OF THE WORKS, and also Reports on the Brooklyn, Hartford, Belleville, and Cambridge Pumping Engines. Prepared and printed by order of the Board of Water Commissioners. With 59 illustrations.

CONTENTS.—Supply Ponds—The Conduit—Ridgewood Engine House and Pump Well—Ridgewood Engines—Force Mains—Ridgewood Reservoir—Pipe Distribution—Mount Prospect Reservoir—Mount Prospect Engine House and Engine—Drainage Grounds—Sewerage Works—Appendix.

Kirkwood on Filtration.

4to. Cloth. $15.00.

REPORT ON THE FILTRATION OF RIVER WATERS, for the Supply of Cities, as practised in Europe, made to the Board of Water Commissioners of the City of St. Louis. By JAMES P. KIRKWOOD. Illustrated by 30 double-plate engravings.

CONTENTS.—Report on Filtration—London Works, General—Chelsea Water Works and Filters—Lambeth Water Works and Filters—Southwark and Vauxhall Water Works and Filters—Grand Junction Water Works and Filters—West Middlesex Water Works and Filters—New River Water Works and Filters—East London Water Works and Filters—Leicester Water Works and Filters—York Water Works and Filters—Liverpool Water Works and Filters—Edinburgh Water Works and Filters—Dublin Water Works and Filters—Perth Water Works and Filtering Gallery—Berlin Water Works and Filters—Hamburg Water Works and Reservoirs—Altona Water Works and Filters—Tours Water Works and Filtering Canal—Angers Water Works and Filtering Galleries—Nantes Water Works and Filters—Lyons Water Works and Filtering Galleries—Toulouse Water Works and Filtering Galleries—Marseilles Water Works and Filters—Genoa Water Works and Filtering Galleries—Leghorn Water Works and Cisterns—Wakefield Water Works and Filters—Appendix.

Tunner on Roll-Turning.

1 vol. 8vo. and 1 vol. plates. $10.00.

A TREATISE ON ROLL-TURNING FOR THE MANUFACTURE OF IRON. By PETER TUNNER. Translated and adapted. By JOHN B. PEARSE, of the Pennsylvania Steel Works. With numerous wood-cuts, 8vo., together with a folio atlas of 10 lithographed plates of Rolls, Measurements, &c.

"We commend this book as a clear, elaborate, and practical treatise upon the department of iron manufacturing operations to which it is devoted. The writer states in his preface, that for twenty-five years he has felt the necessity of such a work, and has evidently brought to its preparation the fruits of experience, a painstaking regard for accuracy of statement, and a desire to furnish information in a style readily understood. The book should be in the hands of every one interested, either in the general practice of mechanical engineering, or the special branch of manufacturing operations to which the work relates.' —*American Artisan.*

Glynn on the Power of Water.

12mo. Cloth. $1.00.

A TREATISE ON THE POWER OF WATER, as applied to drive Flour Mills, and to give motion to Turbines and other Hydrostatic Engines. By JOSEPH GLYNN, F.R. S. Third edition, revised and enlarged, with numerous illustrations.

Hewson on Embankments.

8vo. Cloth. $2.00.

PRINCIPLES AND PRACTICE OF EMBANKING LANDS from River Floods, as applied to the Levees of the Mississippi. By WILLIAM HEWSON, Civil Engineer.

"This is a valuable treatise on the principles and practice of embanking lands from river floods, as applied to the Levees of the Mississippi, by a highly intelligent and experienced engineer. The author says it is a first attempt to reduce to order and to rule the design, execution, and measurement of the Levees of the Mississippi. It is a most useful and needed contribution to scientific literature.—*Philadelphia Evening Journal.*

Grüner on Steel.

8vo. Cloth. $3.50.

THE MANUFACTURE OF STEEL. By M. L. GRUNER, translated from the French. By Lenox Smith, A. M., E. M., with an appendix on the Bessemer Process in the United States, by the translator. Illustrated by lithographed drawings and wood-cuts.

"The purpose of the work is to present a careful, elaborate, and at the same time practical examination into the physical properties of steel, as well as a description of the new processes and mechanical appliances for its manufacture. The information which it contains, gathered from many trustworthy sources, will be found of much value to the American steel manufacturer, who may thus acquaint himself with the results of careful and elaborate experiments in other countries, and better prepare himself for successful competition in this important industry with foreign makers. The fact that this volume is from the pen of one of the ablest metallurgists of the present day, cannot fail, we think, to secure for it a favorable consideration.—*Iron Age.*

Bauerman on Iron.

12mo. Cloth. $2.00.

TREATISE ON THE METALLURGY OF IRON. Containing outlines of the History of Iron Manufacture, methods of Assay, and analysis of Iron Ores, processes of manufacture of Iron and Steel, etc., etc. By H. BAUERMAN. First American edition. Revised and enlarged, with an appendix on the Martin Process for making Steel, from the report of Abram S. Hewitt. Illustrated with numerous wood engravings.

"This is an important addition to the stock of technical works published in this country. It embodies the latest facts, discoveries, and processes connected with the manufacture of iron and steel, and should be in the hands of every person interested in the subject, as well as in all technical and scientific libraries."—*Scientific American.*

Link and Valve Motions, by W. S. Auchincloss.

8vo. Cloth. $3.00.

APPLICATION OF THE SLIDE VALVE and Link Motion to Stationary, Portable, Locomotive and Marine Engines, with new and simple methods for proportioning the parts. By WILLIAM S. AUCHINCLOSS, Civil and Mechanical Engineer. Designed as a hand-book for Mechanical Engineers, Master Mechanics, Draughtsmen and Students of Steam Engineering. All dimensions of the valve are found with the greatest ease by means of a Printed Scale, and proportions of the link determined *without* the assistance of a model. Illustrated by 37 wood-cuts and 21 lithographic plates, together with a copperplate engraving of the Travel Scale.

All the matters we have mentioned are treated with a clearness and absence of unnecessary verbiage which renders the work a peculiarly valuable one. The Travel Scale only requires to be known to be appreciated. Mr. A. writes so ably on his subject, we wish he had written more. *London Engineering.*

We have never opened a work relating to steam which seemed to us better calculated to give an intelligent mind a clear understanding of the department it discusses.—*Scientific American.*

Slide Valve by Eccentrics, by Prof. C. W. MacCord.

4to. Illustrated. Cloth, $4.00.

A PRACTICAL TREATISE ON THE SLIDE VALVE BY ECCENTRICS, examining by methods, the action of the Eccentric upon the Slide Valve, and explaining the practical processes of laying out the movements, adapting the valve for its various duties in the steam-engine. For the use of Engineers, Draughtsmen, Machinists, and Students of valve motions in general. By C. W. MacCord, A. M., Professor of Mechanical Drawing, Stevens' Institute of Technology, Hoboken, N J.

Stillman's Steam-Engine Indicator.

12mo. Cloth. $1.00.

THE STEAM-ENGINE INDICATOR, and the Improved Manometer Steam and Vacuum Gauges; their utility and application By Paul Stillman. New edition.

Bacon's Steam-Engine Indicator.

12mo. Cloth. $1.00. Mor. $1.50.

A TREATISE ON THE RICHARDS STEAM-ENGINE INDICATOR, with directions for its use. By Charles T. Porter. Revised, with notes and large additions as developed by American Practice, with an Appendix containing useful formulæ and rules for Engineers. By F. W. Bacon, M. E., Member of the American Society of Civil Engineers. Illustrated. Second Edition

In this work, Mr. Porter's book has been taken as the basis, but Mr. Bacon has adapted it to American Practice, and has conferred a great boon on American Engineers.—*Artisan.*

Bartol on Marine Boilers.

8vo. Cloth. $1.50.

TREATISE ON THE MARINE BOILERS OF THE UNITED STATES. By H. B. Bartol. Illustrated.

Gillmore's Limes and Cements.

Fourth Edition. Revised and Enlargd.

8vo. Cloth. $4.00.

PRACTICAL TREATISE ON LIMES, HYDRAULIC CEMENTS, AND MORTARS. Papers on Practical Engineering, U. S. Engineer Department, No. 9, containing Reports of numerous experiments conducted in New York City, during the years 1858 to 1861, inclusive. By Q. A. GILLMORE, Brig-General U. S. Volunteers, and Major U. S. Corps of Engineers. With numerous illustrations.

"This work contains a record of certain experiments and researches made under the authority of the Engineer Bureau of the War Department from 1858 to 1861, upon the various hydraulic cements of the United States, and the materials for their manufacture. The experiments were carefully made, and are well reported and compiled.'—*Journal Franklin Institute.*

Gillmore's Coignet Beton.

8vo. Cloth. $2.50.

COIGNET BETON AND OTHER ARTIFICIAL STONE. By Q. A. GILLMORE. 9 Plates, Views, etc.

This work describes with considerable minuteness of detail the several kinds of artificial stone in most general use in Europe and now beginning to be introduced in the United States, discusses their properties, relative merits, and cost, and describes the materials of which they are composed. . . . . The subject is one of special and growing interest, and we commend the work, embodying as it does the matured opinions of an experienced engineer and expert.

Williamson's Practical Tables.

4to. Flexible Cloth. $2.50.

PRACTICAL TABLES IN METEOROLOGY AND HYPSOMETRY, in connection with the use of the Barometer. By Col. R. S. WILLIAMSOM, U. S. A.

Williamson on the Barometer.

4to. Cloth. $15.00.

ON THE USE OF THE BAROMETER ON SURVEYS AND RECONNAISSANCES. Part I. Meteorology in its Connection with Hypsometry. Part II. Barometric Hypsometry. By R. S. WILLIAMSON, Bvt. Lieut.-Col. U. S. A., Major Corps of Engineers. With Illustrative Tables and Engravings. Paper No. 15, Professional Papers, Corps of Engineers.

"SAN FRANCISCO, CAL., *Feb.* 27, 1867.

"Gen. A. A. HUMPHREYS, Chief of Engineers, U. S. Army:

"GENERAL,—I have the honor to submit to you, in the following pages, the results of my investigations in meteorology and hypsometry, made with the view of ascertaining how far the barometer can be used as a reliable instrument for determining altitudes on extended lines of survey and reconnaissances. These investigations have occupied the leisure permitted me from my professional duties during the last ten years, and I hope the results will be deemed of sufficient value to have a place assigned them among the printed professional papers of the United States Corps of Engineers.

"Very respectfully, your obedient servant,

"R. S. WILLIAMSON,

"Bvt. Lt.-Col. U. S. A., Major Corps of U. S. Engineers."

Von Cotta's Ore Deposits.

8vo. Cloth. $4.00.

TREATISE ON ORE DEPOSITS. By BERNHARD VON COTTA, Professor of Geology in the Royal School of Mines, Freidberg, Saxony. Translated from the second German edition, by FREDERICK PRIME, Jr., Mining Engineer, and revised by the author, with numerous illustrations.

"Prof. Von Cotta of the Freiberg School of Mines, is the author of the best modern treatise on ore deposits, and we are heartily glad that this admirable work has been translated and published in this country. The translator, Mr. Frederick Prime, Jr., a graduate of Freiberg, has had in his work the great advantage of a revision by the author himself, who declares in a prefatory note that this may be considered as a new edition (the third) of his own book.

"It is a timely and welcome contribution to the literature of mining in this country, and we are grateful to the translator for his enterprise and good judgment in undertaking its preparation; while we recognize with equal cordiality the liberality of the author in granting both permission and assistance."—*Extract from Review in Engineering and Mining Journal.*

Plattner's Blow-Pipe Analysis.

Second edition. Revised. 8vo. Cloth. $7.50.

PLATTNER'S MANUAL OF QUALITATIVE AND QUANTITATIVE ANALYSIS WITH THE BLOW-PIPE. From the last German edition Revised and enlarged. By Prof. TH. RICHTER, of the Royal Saxon Mining Academy. Translated by Prof. H. B. CORNWALL, Assistant in the Columbia School of Mines, New York; assisted by JOHN H. CASWELL. Illustrated with eighty-seven wood-cuts and one Lithographic Plate. 560 pages.

"Plattner's celebrated work has long been recognized as the only complete book on Blow-Pipe Analysis. The fourth German edition, edited by Prof. Richter, fully sustains the reputation which the earlier editions acquired during the lifetime of the author, and it is a source of great satisfaction to us to know that Prof. Richter has co-operated with the translator in issuing the American edition of the work, which is in fact a fifth edition of the original work, being far more complete than the last German edition."—*Silliman's Journal.*

There is nothing so complete to be found in the English language. Plattner's book is not a mere pocket edition; it is intended as a comprehensive guide to all that is at present known on the blow-pipe, and as such is really indispensable to teachers and advanced pupils.

"Mr. Cornwall's edition is something more than a translation, as it contains many corrections, emendations and additions not to be found in the original. It is a decided improvement on the work in its German dress."—*Journal of Applied Chemistry.*

Egleston's Mineralogy.

8vo. Illustrated with 34 Lithographic Plates. Cloth. $4.50.

LECTURES ON DESCRIPTIVE MINERALOGY, Delivered at the School of Mines, Columbia College. BY PROFESSOR T. EGLESTON.

These lectures are what their title indicates, the lectures on Mineralogy delivered at the School of Mines of Columbia College. They have been printed for the students, in order that more time might be given to the various methods of examining and determining minerals. The second part has only been printed. The first part, comprising crystallography and physical mineralogy, will be printed at some future time.

Pynchon's Chemical Physics.

New Edition. Revised and Enlarged.

Crown 8vo. Cloth. $3.00.

INTRODUCTION TO CHEMICAL PHYSICS, Designed for the Use of Academies, Colleges, and High Schools. Illustrated with numerous engravings, and containing copious experiments with directions for preparing them. By THOMAS RUGGLES PYNCHON, M.A., Professor of Chemistry and the Natural Sciences, Trinity College, Hartford.

Hitherto, no work suitable for general use, treating of all these subjects within the limits of a single volume, could be found; consequently the attention they have received has not been at all proportionate to their importance. It is believed that a book containing so much valuable information within so small a compass, cannot fail to meet with a ready sale among all intelligent persons, while Professional men, Physicians, Medical Students, Photographers, Telegraphers, Engineers, and Artisans generally, will find it specially valuable, if not nearly indispensable, as a book of reference.

"We strongly recommend this able treatise to our readers as the first work ever published on the subject free from perplexing technicalities. In style it is pure, in description graphic, and its typographical appearance is artistic. It is altogether a most excellent work."—*Eclectic Medical Journal.*

"It treats fully of Photography, Telegraphy, Steam Engines, and the various applications of Electricity. In short, it is a carefully prepared volume, abreast with the latest scientific discoveries and inventions."—*Hartford Courant.*

Plympton's Blow-Pipe Analysis.

12mo. Cloth. $2.00.

THE BLOW-PIPE: A System of Instruction in its practical use being a graduated course of Analysis for the use of students, and all those engaged in the Examination of Metallic Combinations. Second edition, with an appendix and a copious index. By GEORGE W. PLYMPTON, of the Polytechnic Institute, Brooklyn.

"This manual probably has no superior in the English language as a text-book for beginners, or as a guide to the student working without a teacher. To the latter many illustrations of the utensils and apparatus required in using the blow-pipe, as well as the fully illustrated description of the blow-pipe flame, will be especially serviceable."—*New York Teacher.*

Ure's Dictionary.

Sixth Edition.

London, 1872.

3 vols. 8vo. Cloth, $25.00. Half Russia, $32.50.

DICTIONARY OF ARTS, MANUFACTURES, AND MINES. By ANDREW URE, M.D. Sixth edition. Edited by ROBERT HUNT, F.R.S., greatly enlarged and rewritten.

Brande and Cox's Dictionary.

New Edition.

London, 1872.

3 vols. 8vo. Cloth, $20.00. Half Morocco, $27.50.

A Dictionary of Science, Literature, and Art. Edited by W. T. BRANDE and Rev. GEO. W. COX. New and enlarged edition.

Watt's Dictionary of Chemistry.

Supplementary Volume.

8vo. Cloth. $9.00.

This volume brings the Record of Chemical Discovery down to the end of the year 1869, including also several additions to, and corrections of, former results which have appeared in 1870 and 1871.

*** Complete Sets of the Work, New and Revised edition, including above supplement. 6 vols. 8vo. Cloth. $62.00.

Rammelsberg's Chemical Analysis.

8vo. Cloth. $2.25.

GUIDE TO A COURSE OF QUANTITATIVE CHEMICAL ANALYSIS, ESPECIALLY OF MINERALS AND FURNACE PRODUCTS. Illustrated by Examples. By C. F. RAMMELSBERG. Translated by J. TOWLER, M.D.

This work has been translated, and is now published expressly for those students in chemistry whose time and other studies in colleges do not permit them to enter upon the more elaborate and expensive treatises of Fresenius and others. It is the condensed labor of a master in chemistry and of a practical analyst.

Eliot and Storer's Qualitative Chemical Analysis.

New Edition, Revised.

12mo. Illustrated. Cloth. $1.50.

A COMPENDIOUS MANUAL OF QUALITATIVE CHEMICAL ANALYSIS. By CHARLES W. ELIOT and FRANK H. STORER. Revised with the Coöperation of the Authors, by WILLIAM RIPLEY NICHOLS, Professor of Chemistry in the Massachusetts Institute of Technology.

"This Manual has great merits as a practical introduction to the science and the art of which it treats. It contains enough of the theory and practice of qualitative analysis, "in the wet way," to bring out all the reasoning involved in the science, and to present clearly to the student the most approved methods of the art. It is specially adapted for exercises and experiments in the laboratory; and yet its classifications and manner of treatment are so systematic and logical throughout, as to adapt it in a high degree to that higher class of students generally who desire an accurate knowledge of the practical methods of arriving at scientific facts."—*Lutheran Observer.*

"We wish every academical class in the land could have the benefit of the fifty exercises of two hours each necessary to master this book. Chemistry would cease to be a mere matter of memory, and become a pleasant experimental and intellectual recreation. We heartily commend this little volume to the notice of those teachers who believe in using the sciences as means of mental discipline."—*College Courant.*

Craig's Decimal System.

Square 32mo. Limp. 50c.

WEIGHTS AND MEASURES. An Account of the Decimal System, with Tables of Conversion for Commercial and Scientific Uses. By B. F. CRAIG, M. D.

"The most lucid, accurate, and useful of all the hand-books on this subject that we have yet seen. It gives forty-seven tables of comparison between the English and French denominations of length, area, capacity, weight, and the Centigrade and Fahrenheit thermometers, with clear instructions how to use them; and to this practical portion, which helps to make the transition as easy as possible, is prefixed a scientific explanation of the errors in the metric system, and how they may be corrected in the laboratory."—*Nation.*

Nugent on Optics.

12mo. Cloth. $2.00

TREATISE ON OPTICS; or, Light and Sight, theoretically and practically treated; with the application to Fine Art and Industrial Pursuits. By E. NUGENT. With one hundred and three illustrations.

"This book is of a practical rather than a theoretical kind, and is designed to afford accurate and complete information to all interested in applications of the science."—*Round Table.*

Barnard's Metric System.

8vo. Brown cloth. $3.00.

THE METRIC SYSTEM OF WEIGHTS AND MEASURES. An Address delivered before the Convocation of the University of the State of New York, at Albany, August, 1871. By FREDERICK A. P. BARNARD, President of Columbia College, New York City. Second edition from the Revised edition printed for the Trustees of Columbia College. Tinted paper.

"It is the best summary of the arguments in favor of the metric weights and measures with which we are acquainted, not only because it contains in small space the leading facts of the case, but because it puts the advocacy of that system on the only tenable grounds, namely, the great convenience of a decimal notation of weight and measure as well as money, the value of international uniformity in the matter, and the fact that this metric system is adopted and in general use by the majority of civilized nations."—*The Nation.*

The Young Mechanic.

Illustrated. 12mo. Cloth. $1.75.

THE YOUNG MECHANIC. Containing directions for the use of all kinds of tools, and for the construction of steam engines and mechanical models, including the Art of Turning in Wood and Metal. By the author of "The Lathe and its Uses," etc. From the English edition, with corrections.

Harrison's Mechanic's Tool-Book.

12mo. Cloth. $1.50.

MECHANIC'S TOOL BOOK, with practical rules and suggestions, for the use of Machinists, Iron Workers, and others. By W. B. Harrison, Associate Editor of the "American Artisan." Illustrated with 44 engravings.

"This work is specially adapted to meet the wants of Machinists and workers in iron generally. It is made up of the work-day experience of an intelligent and ingenious mechanic, who had the faculty of adapting tools to various purposes. The practicability of his plans and suggestions are made apparent even to the unpractised eye by a series of well-executed wood engravings."—*Philadelphia Inquirer.*

Pope's Modern Practice of the Electric Telegraph.

Eighth Edition. 8vo. Cloth $2.00.

A Hand-book for Electricians and Operators. By Frank L. Pope. Seventh edition. Revised and enlarged, and fully illustrated.

Extract from Letter of Prof. Morse.

"I have had time only cursorily to examine its contents, but this examination has resulted in great gratification, especially at the fairness and unprejudiced tone of your whole work.

"Your illustrated diagrams are admirable and beautifully executed.

"I think all your instructions in the use of the telegraph apparatus judicious and correct, and I most cordially wish you success."

Extract from Letter of Prof. G. W. Hough, of the Dudley Observatory.

"There is no other work of this kind in the English language that contains in so small a compass so much practical information in the application of galvanic electricity to telegraphy. It should be in the hands of every one interested in telegraphy, or the use of Batteries for other purposes."

Morse's Telegraphic Apparatus.

Illustrated. 8vo. Cloth. $2.00.

EXAMINATION OF THE TELEGRAPHIC APPARATUS AND THE PROCESSES IN TELEGAPHY. By Samuel F. B. Morse, LL.D., United States Commissioner Paris Universal Exposition, 1867.

Sabine's History of the Telegraph.

12mo. Cloth. $1.25.

HISTORY AND PROGRESS OF THE ELECTRIC TELEGRAPH, with Descriptions of some of the Apparatus. By ROBERT SABINE, C. E. Second edition, with additions.

CONTENTS.—I. Early Observations of Electrical Phenomena. II. Telegraphs by Frictional Electricity. III. Telegraphs by Voltaic Electricity. IV. Telegraphs by Electro-Magnetism and Magneto-Electricity. V. Telegraphs now in use. VI. Overhead Lines. VII. Submarine Telegraph Lines. VIII. Underground Telegraphs. IX. Atmospheric Electricity.

Haskins' Galvanometer.

Pocket form. Illustrated. Morocco tucks. $2.00.

THE GALVANOMETER, AND ITS USES; a Manual for Electricians and Students. By C. H. HASKINS.

"We hope this excellent little work will meet with the sale its merits entitle it to. To every telegrapher who owns, or uses a Galvanometer, or ever expects to, it will be quite indispensable."—*The Telegrapher.*

Culley's Hand-Book of Telegraphy.

8vo. Cloth. $6.00.

A HAND-BOOK OF PRACTICAL TELEGRAPHY. By R. S. CULLEY, Engineer to the Electric and International Telegraph Company. Fifth edition, revised and enlarged.

Foster's Submarine Blasting.

4to. Cloth. $3.50.

SUBMARINE BLASTING in Boston Harbor, Massachusetts—Removal of Tower and Corwin Rocks. By JOHN G. FOSTER, Lieutenant-Colonel of Engineers, and Brevet Major-General, U. S. Army. Illustrated with seven plates.

LIST OF PLATES.—1. Sketch of the Narrows, Boston Harbor. 2. Townsend's Submarine Drilling Machine, and Working Vessel attending. 3. Submarine Drilling Machine employed. 4. Details of Drilling Machine employed. 5. Cartridges and Tamping used. 6. Fuses and Insulated Wires used. 7. Portable Friction Battery used.

Barnes' Submarine Warfare.

8vo. Cloth. $5.00.

SUBMARINE WARFARE, DEFENSIVE AND OFFENSIVE. Comprising a full and complete History of the Invention of the Torpedo, its employment in War and results of its use. Descriptions of the various forms of Torpedoes, Submarine Batteries and Torpedo Boats actually used in War. Methods of Ignition by Machinery, Contact Fuzes, and Electricity, and a full account of experiments made to determine the Explosive Force of Gunpowder under Water. Also a discussion of the Offensive Torpedo system, its effect upon Iron-Clad Ship systems, and influence upon Future Naval Wars. By Lieut.-Commander JOHN S. BARNES, U. S. N. With twenty lithographic plates and many wood-cuts.

"A book important to military men, and especially so to engineers and artillerists. It consists of an examination of the various offensive and defensive engines that have been contrived for submarine hostilities, including a discussion of the torpedo system, its effects upon iron-clad ship-systems, and its probable influence upon future naval wars. Plates of a valuable character accompany the treatise, which affords a useful history of the momentous subject it discusses. A great deal of useful information is collected in its pages, especially concerning the inventions of SCHOLL and VERDU, and of JONES' and HUNT'S batteries, as well as of other similar machines, and the use in submarine operations of gun-cotton and nitro-glycerine."—*N. Y. Times.*

Randall's Quartz Operator's Hand-Book.

12mo. Cloth. $2.00.

QUARTZ OPERATOR'S HAND-BOOK. By P. M. RANDALL. New edition, revised and enlarged. Fully illustrated.

The object of this work has been to present a clear and comprehensive exposition of mineral veins, and the means and modes chiefly employed for the mining and working of their ores—more especially those containing gold and silver.

Mitchell's Manual of Assaying.

8vo. Cloth. $10.00.

A MANUAL OF PRACTICAL ASSAYING. By JOHN MITCHELL. Third edition. Edited by WILLIAM CROOKES, F.R.S.

In this edition are incorporated all the late important discoveries in Assaying made in this country and abroad, and special care is devoted to the very important Volumetric and Colorimetric Assays, as well as to the Blow-Pipe Assays.

Benét's Chronoscope.

Second Edition.

Illustrated. 4to. Cloth. $3.00.

ELECTRO-BALLISTIC MACHINES, and the Schultz Chronoscope. By Lieutenant-Colonel S. V. BENÉT, Captain of Ordnance, U. S. Army.

CONTENTS.—1. Ballistic Pendulum. 2. Gun Pendulum. 3. Use of Electricity. 4. Navez' Machine. 5. Vignotti's Machine, with Plates. 6. Benton's Electro-Ballistic Pendulum, with Plates. 7. Leur's Tro-Pendulum Machine 8. Schultz's Chronoscope, with two Plates.

Michaelis' Chronograph.

4to. Illustrated. Cloth. $3.00.

THE LE BOULENGÉ CHRONOGRAPH. With three lithographed folding plates of illustrations. By Brevet Captain O E. MICHAELIS, First Lieutenant Ordnance Corps, U. S. Army.

"The excellent monograph of Captain Michaelis enters minutely into the details of construction and management, and gives tables of the times of flight calculated upon a given fall of the chronometer for all distances. Captain Michaelis has done good service in presenting this work to his brother officers, describing, as it does, an instrument which bids fair to be in constant use in our future ballistic experiments.' —*Army and Navy Journal.*

Silversmith's Hand-Book.

Fourth Edition.

Illustrated. 12mo. Cloth. $3.00.

A PRACTICAL HAND-BOOK FOR MINERS, Metallurgists, and Assayers, comprising the most recent improvements in the disintegration, amalgamation, smelting, and parting of the Precious Ores, with a Comprehensive Digest of the Mining Laws. Greatly augmented, revised, and corrected. By JULIUS SILVERSMITH. Fourth edition. Profusely illustrated. 1 vol. 12mo. Cloth. $3.00.

One of the most important features of this work is that in which the metallurgy of the precious metals is treated of. In it the author has endeavored to embody all the processes for the reduction and manipulation of the precious ores heretofore successfully employed in Germany, England, Mexico, and the United States, together with such as have been more recently invented, and not yet fully tested—all of which are profusely illustrated and easy of comprehension.

Simms' Levelling.

8vo. Cloth. $2.50.

A TREATISE ON THE PRINCIPLES AND PRACTICE OF LEVELLING, showing its application to purposes of Railway Engineering and the Construction of Roads, &c. By FREDERICK W. SIMMS, C. E. From the fifth London edition, revised and corrected, with the addition of Mr. Law's Practical Examples for Setting Out Railway Curves. Illustrated with three lithographic plates and numerous wood-cuts.

"One of the most important text-books for the general surveyor, and there is scarcely a question connected with levelling for which a solution would be sought, but that would be satisfactorily answered by consulting this volume." —*Mining Journal.*

"The text-book on levelling in most of our engineering schools and colleges."—*Engineers.*

"The publishers have rendered a substantial service to the profession, especially to the younger members, by bringing out the present edition of Mr. Simms' useful work."—*Engineering.*

Stuart's Successful Engineer.

18mo. Boards. 50 cents.

HOW TO BECOME A SUCCESSFUL ENGINEER: Being Hints to Youths intending to adopt the Profession. By BERNARD STUART, Engineer. Sixth Edition.

"A valuable little book of sound, sensible advice to young men who wish to rise in the most important of the professions."—*Scientific American.*

Stuart's Naval Dry Docks.

Twenty-four engravings on steel.

Fourth Edition.

4to. Cloth. $6.00.

THE NAVAL DRY DOCKS OF THE UNITED STATES. By CHARLES B. STUART. Engineer in Chief of the United States Navy.

List of Illustrations.

Pumping Engine and Pumps—Plan of Dry Dock and Pump-Well—Sections of Dry Dock—Engine House—Iron Floating Gate—Details of Floating Gate—Iron Turning Gate—Plan of Turning Gate—Culvert Gate—Filling Culvert Gates—Engine Bed—Plate, Pumps, and Culvert—Engine House Roof—Floating Sectional Dock—Details of Section, and Plan of Turn-Tables—Plan of Basin and Marine Railways—Plan of Sliding Frame, and Elevation of Pumps—Hydraulic Cylinder—Plan of Gearing for Pumps and End Floats—Perspective View of Dock, Basin, and Railway—Plan of Basin of Portsmouth Dry Dock—Floating Balance Dock—Elevation of Trusses and the Machinery—Perspective View of Balance Dry Dock

---

Free Hand Drawing.

Profusely Illustrated. 18mo. Boards. 50 cents.

A GUIDE TO ORNAMENTAL, Figure, and Landscape Drawing. By an Art Student.

CONTENTS.—Materials employed in Drawing, and how to use them—On Lines and how to Draw them—On Shading—Concerning lines and shading, with applications of them to simple elementary subjects—Sketches from Nature.

Minifie's Mechanical Drawing.

Eighth Edition.

Royal 8vo. Cloth. $4.00.

A TEXT-BOOK OF GEOMETRICAL DRAWING for the use of Mechanics and Schools, in which the Definitions and Rules of Geometry are familiarly explained; the Practical Problems are arranged, from the most simple to the more complex, and in their description technicalities are avoided as much as possible. With illustrations for Drawing Plans, Sections, and Elevations of Buildings and Machinery; an Introduction to Isometrical Drawing, and an Essay on Linear Perspective and Shadows. Illustrated with over 200 diagrams engraved on steel. By WM. MINIFIE, Architect. Eighth Edition. With an Appendix on the Theory and Application of Colors.

"It is the best work on Drawing that we have ever seen, and is especially a text-book of Geometrical Drawing for the use of Mechanics and Schools. No young Mechanic, such as a Machinist, Engineer, Cabinet-Maker, Millwright, or Carpenter, should be without it."—*Scientific American.*

"One of the most comprehensive works of the kind ever published, and cannot but possess great value to builders. The style is at once elegant and substantial."—*Pennsylvania Inquirer.*

"Whatever is said is rendered perfectly intelligible by remarkably well-executed diagrams on steel, leaving nothing for mere vague supposition; and the addition of an introduction to isometrical drawing, linear perspective, and the projection of shadows, winding up with a useful index to technical terms."—*Glasgow Mechanics' Journal.*

☞ The British Government has authorized the use of this book in their schools of art at Somerset House, London, and throughout the kingdom.

Minifie's Geometrical Drawing.

New Edition. Enlarged.

12mo. Cloth. $2.00.

GEOMETRICAL DRAWING. Abridged from the octavo edition, for the use of Schools. Illustrated with 48 steel plates. New edition, enlarged.

"It is well adapted as a text-book of drawing to be used in our High Schools and Academies where this useful branch of the fine arts has been hitherto too much neglected."—*Boston Journal.*

Bell on Iron Smelting.

8vo. Cloth. $6.00.

CHEMICAL PHENOMENA OF IRON SMELTING. An experimental and practical examination of the circumstances which determine the capacity of the Blast Furnace, the Temperature of the Air, and the Proper Condition of the Materials to be operated upon. By I. LOWTHIAN BELL.

"The reactions which take place in every foot of the blast-furnace have been investigated, and the nature of every step in the process, from the introduction of the raw material into the furnace to the production of the pig iron, has been carefully ascertained, and recorded so fully that any one in the trade can readily avail themselves of the knowledge acquired; and we have no hesitation in saying that the judicious application of such knowledge will do much to facilitate the introduction of arrangements which will still further economize fuel, and at the same time permit of the quality of the resulting metal being maintained, if not improved. The volume is one which no practical pig iron manufacturer can afford to be without if he be desirous of entering upon that competition which nowadays is essential to progress, and in issuing such a work Mr. Bell has entitled himself to the best thanks of every member of the trade."—*London Mining Journal.*

King's Notes on Steam.

Thirteenth Edition.

8vo. Cloth. $2.00.

LESSONS AND PRACTICAL NOTES ON STEAM, the Steam-Engine, Propellers, &c., &c., for Young Engineers, Students, and others. By the late W. R. KING, U. S. N. Revised by Chief-Engineer J. W. KING, U. S. Navy.

"This is one of the best, because eminently plain and practical treatises on the Steam Engine ever published.'—*Philadelphia Press.*

This is the thirteenth edition of a valuable work of the late W. H. King, U. S. N. It contains lessons and practical notes on Steam and the Steam Engine, Propellers, etc. It is calculated to be of great use to young marine engineers, students, and others. The text is illustrated and explained by numerous diagrams and representations of machinery.—*Boston Daily Advertiser.*

Text-book at the U. S. Naval Academy, Annapolis.

Burgh's Modern Marine Engineering.

One thick 4to vol. Cloth. $25.00. Half morocco. $30.00.

MODERN MARINE ENGINEERING, applied to Paddle and Screw Propulsion. Consisting of 36 Colored Plates, 259 Practical Wood-cut Illustrations, and 403 pages of Descriptive Matter, the whole being an exposition of the present practice of the following firms: Messrs. J. Penn & Sons; Messrs. Maudslay, Sons & Field; Messrs. James Watt & Co.; Messrs. J. & G. Rennie; Messrs. R. Napier & Sons; Messrs. J. & W. Dudgeon; Messrs. Ravenhill & Hodgson; Messrs. Humphreys & Tenant; Mr. J. T. Spencer, and Messrs. Forrester & Co. By N. P. BURGH, Engineer.

PRINCIPAL CONTENTS.—General Arrangements of Engines, 11 examples—General Arrangement of Boilers, 14 examples—General Arrangement of Superheaters, 11 examples—Details of Oscillating Paddle Engines, 34 examples—Condensers for Screw Engines, both Injection and Surface, 20 examples—Details of Screw Engines, 20 examples—Cylinders and Details of Screw Engines, 21 examples—Slide Valves and Details, 7 examples—Slide Valve, Link Motion, 7 examples—Expansion Valves and Gear, 10 examples—Details in General, 30 examples—Screw Propeller and Fittings, 13 examples—Engine and Boiler Fittings, 28 examples—In relation to the Principles of the Marine Engine and Boiler, 33 examples.

Notices of the Press.

"Every conceivable detail of the Marine Engine, under all its various forms, is profusely, and we must add, admirably illustrated by a multitude of engravings, selected from the best and most modern practice of the first Marine Engineers of the day. The chapter on Condensers is peculiarly valuable. In one word, there is no other work in existence which will bear a moment's comparison with it as an exponent of the skill, talent and practical experience to which is due the splendid reputation enjoyed by many British Marine Engineers."—*Engineer.*

"This very comprehensive work, which was issued in Monthly parts, has just been completed. It contains large and full drawings and copious descriptions of most of the best examples of Modern Marine Engines, and it is a complete theoretical and practical treatise on the subject of Marine Engineering."—*American Artisan.*

This is the only edition of the above work with the beautifully *colored* plates, and it is out of print in England.

Bourne's Treatise on the Steam Engine.

Ninth Edition.

Illustrated. 4to. Cloth. $15.00.

TREATISE ON THE STEAM ENGINE in its various applications to Mines, Mills, Steam Navigation, Railways, and Agriculture, with the theoretical investigations respecting the Motive Power of Heat and the proper Proportions of Steam Engines. Elaborate Tables of the right dimensions of every part, and Practical Instructions for the Manufacture and Management of every species of Engine in actual use. By JOHN BOURNE, being the ninth edition of "A Treatise on the Steam Engine," by the "Artisan Club." Illustrated by thirty-eight plates and five hundred and forty-six wood-cuts.

As Mr. Bourne's work has the great merit of avoiding unsound and immature views, it may safely be consulted by all who are really desirous of acquiring trustworthy information on the subject of which it treats. During the twenty-two years which have elapsed from the issue of the first edition, the improvements introduced in the construction of the steam engine have been both numerous and important, and of these Mr. Bourne has taken care to point out the more prominent, and to furnish the reader with such information as shall enable him readily to judge of their relative value. This edition has been thoroughly modernized, and made to accord with the opinions and practice of the more successful engineers of the present day. All that the book professes to give is given with ability and evident care. The scientific principles which are permanent are admirably explained, and reference is made to many of the more valuable of the recently introduced engines. To express an opinion of the value and utility of such a work as *The Artisan Club's Treatise on the Steam Engine*, which has passed through eight editions already, would be superfluous; but it may be safely stated that the work is worthy the attentive study of all either engaged in the manufacture of steam engines or interested in economizing the use of steam.—*Mining Journal.*

Isherwood's Engineering Precedents.

Two Vols. in One. 8vo. Cloth. $2.50.

ENGINEERING PRECEDENTS FOR STEAM MACHINERY. Arranged in the most practical and useful manner for Engineers. By B. F. ISHERWOOD, Civil Engineer, U. S. Navy. With illustrations.

Ward's Steam for the Million.

New and Revised Edition.

8vo. Cloth. $1.00.

STEAM FOR THE MILLION. A Popular Treatise on Steam and its Application to the Useful Arts, especially to Navigation. By J. H. WARD, Commander U. S. Navy. New and revised edition.

A most excellent work for the young engineer and general reader. Many facts relating to the management of the boiler and engine are set forth with a simplicity of language and perfection of detail that bring the subject home to the reader.—*American Engineer.*

Walker's Screw Propulsion.

8vo. Cloth. 75 cents.

NOTES ON SCREW PROPULSION, its Rise and History. By Capt. W. H. WALKER, U. S. Navy.

Commander Walker's book contains an immense amount of concise practical data, and every item of information recorded fully proves that the various points bearing upon it have been well considered previously to expressing an opinion.—*London Mining Journal.*

Page's Earth's Crust.

18mo. Cloth. 75 cents.

THE EARTH'S CRUST: a Handy Outline of Geology. By DAVID PAGE.

"Such a work as this was much wanted—a work giving in clear and intelligible outline the leading facts of the science, without amplification or irksome details. It is admirable in arrangement, and clear and easy, and, at the same time, forcible in style. It will lead, we hope, to the introduction of Geology into many schools that have neither time nor room for the study of large treatises."—*The Museum.*

Rogers' Geology of Pennsylvania.

3 Vols. 4to, with Portfolio of Maps. Cloth. $30.00.

THE GEOLOGY OF PENNSYLVANIA. A Government Survey. With a general view of the Geology of the United States, Essays on the Coal Formation and its Fossils, and a description of the Coal Fields of North America and Great Britain. By HENRY DARWIN ROGERS, Late State Geologist of Pennsylvania. Splendidly illustrated with Plates and Engravings in the Text.

It certainly should be in every public library throughout the country, and likewise in the possession of all students of Geology. After the final sale of these copies, the work will, of course, become more valuable.

The work for the last five years has been entirely out of the market, but a few copies that remained in the hands of Prof. Rogers, in Scotland, at the time of his death, are now offered to the public, at a price which is even below what it was originally sold for when first published.

Morfit on Pure Fertilizers.

With 28 Illustrative Plates. 8vo. Cloth. $20.00.

A PRACTICAL TREATISE ON PURE FERTILIZERS, and the Chemical Conversion of Rock Guanos, Marlstones, Coprolites, and the Crude Phosphates of Lime and Alumina Generally, into various Valuable Products. By CAMPBELL MORFIT, M.D., F.C.S.

Sweet's Report on Coal.

8vo. Cloth. $3.00.

SPECIAL REPORT ON COAL; showing its Distribution, Classification, and Cost delivered over different routes to various points in the State of New York, and the principal cities on the Atlantic Coast. By S. H. SWEET. With maps.

Colburn's Gas Works of London.

12mo. Boards. 60 cents.

GAS WORKS OF LONDON. By ZERAH COLBURN.

The Useful Metals and their Alloys; Scoffren, Truran, and others.

Fifth Edition.

8vo. Half calf. $3.75.

THE USEFUL METALS AND THEIR ALLOYS, including MINING VENTILATION, MINING JURISPRUDENCE AND METALLURGIC CHEMISTRY employed in the conversion of IRON, COPPER, TIN, ZINC, ANTIMONY, AND LEAD ORES, with their applications to THE INDUSTRIAL ARTS. By JOHN SCOFFREN, WILLIAM TRURAN, WILLIAM CLAY, ROBERT OXLAND, WILLIAM FAIRBAIRN, W. C. AITKIN, and WILLIAM VOSE PICKETT.

Collins' Useful Alloys.

18mo. Flexible. 75 cents.

THE PRIVATE BOOK OF USEFUL ALLOYS and Memoranda for Goldsmiths, Jewellers, etc. By JAMES E. COLLINS

This little book is compiled from notes made by the Author from the papers of one of the largest and most eminent Manufacturing Goldsmiths and Jewellers in this country, and as the firm is now no longer in existence, and the Author is at present engaged in some other undertaking, he now offers to the public the benefit of his experience, and in so doing he begs to state that all the alloys, etc., given in these pages may be confidently relied on as being thoroughly practicable.

The Memoranda and Receipts throughout this book are also compiled from practice, and will no doubt be found useful to the practical jeweller. —*Shirley, July,* 1871.

Joynson's Metals Used in Construction.

12mo. Cloth. 75 cents.

THE METALS USED IN CONSTRUCTION: Iron, Steel, Bessemer Metal, etc., etc. By FRANCIS HERBERT JOYNSON. Illustrated.

"In the interests of practical science, we are bound to notice this work; and to those who wish further information, we should say, buy it; and the outlay, we honestly believe, will be considered well spent." —*Scientific Review.*

Holley's Ordnance and Armor.

493 Engravings. Half Roan, $10.00. Half Russia, $12.00.

A TREATISE ON ORDNANCE AND ARMOR—Embracing Descriptions, Discussions, and Professional Opinions concerning the MATERIAL, FABRICATION, Requirements, Capabilities, and Endurance of European and American Guns, for Naval, Sea Coast, and Iron-clad Warfare, and their RIFLING, PROJECTILES, and BREECH-LOADING; also, Results of Experiments against Armor, from Official Records, with an Appendix referring to Gun-Cotton, Hooped Guns, etc., etc. By ALEXANDER L. HOLLEY, B. P. 948 pages, 493 Engravings, and 147 Tables of Results, etc.

CONTENTS.

Peirce's Analytic Mechanics.

4to. Cloth. $10.00.

SYSTEM OF ANALYTIC MECHANICS. Physical and Celestial Mechanics. By BENJAMIN PEIRCE, Perkins Professor of Astronomy and Mathematics in Harvard University, and Consulting Astronomer of the American Ephemeris and Nautical Almanac. Developed in four systems of Analytic Mechanics, Celestial Mechanics, Potential Physics, and Analytic Morphology.

"I have re-examined the memoirs of the great geometers, and have striven to consolidate their latest researches and their most exalted forms of thought into a consistent and uniform treatise. If I have hereby succeeded in opening to the students of my country a readier access to these choice jewels of intellect; if their brilliancy is not impaired in this attempt to reset them; if, in their own constellation, they illustrate each other, and concentrate a stronger light upon the names of their discoverers, and, still more, if any gem which I may have presumed to add is not wholly lustreless in the collection, I shall feel that my work has not been in vain."—*Extract from the Preface.*

Burt's Key to Solar Compass.

Second Edition.

Pocket Book Form. Tuck. $2.50.

KEY TO THE SOLAR COMPASS, and Surveyor's Companion; comprising all the Rules necessary for use in the field; also, Description of the Linear Surveys and Public Land System of the United States, Notes on the Barometer, Suggestions for an outfit for a Survey of four months, etc., etc., etc. By W. A. BURT, U. S. Deputy Surveyor. Second edition.

Chauvenet's Lunar Distances.

8vo. Cloth. $2.00.

NEW METHOD OF CORRECTING LUNAR DISTANCES, and Improved Method of Finding the Error and Rate of a Chronometer, by equal altitudes. By WM. CHAUVENET, LL.D., Chancellor of Washington University of St. Louis.

Jeffers' Nautical Surveying.

Illustrated with 9 Copperplates and 31 Wood-cut Illustrations. 8vo. Cloth. $5.00.

NAUTICAL SURVEYING. By WILLIAM N. JEFFERS, Captain U. S. Navy.

Many books have been written on each of the subjects treated of in the sixteen chapters of this work; and, to obtain a complete knowledge of geodetic surveying requires a profound study of the whole range of mathematical and physical sciences; but a year of preparation should render any intelligent officer competent to conduct a nautical survey.

CONTENTS.—Chapter I. Formulæ and Constants Useful in Surveying II. Distinctive Character of Surveys. III. Hydrographic Surveying under Sail; or, Running Survey. IV. Hydrographic Surveying of Boats; or, Harbor Survey. V. Tides—Definition of Tidal Phenomena—Tidal Observations. VI. Measurement of Bases—Appropriate and Direct. VII. Measurement of the Angles of Triangles—Azimuths—Astronomical Bearings. VIII. Corrections to be Applied to the Observed Angles. IX. Levelling—Difference of Level. X. Computation of the Sides of the Triangulation—The Three-point Problem. XI. Determination of the Geodetic Latitudes, Longitudes, and Azimuths, of Points of a Triangulation. XII. Summary of Subjects treated of in preceding Chapters—Examples of Computation by various Formulæ. XIII. Projection of Charts and Plans. XIV. Astronomical Determination of Latitude and Longitude. XV. Magnetic Observations. XVI. Deep Sea Soundings. XVII. Tables for Ascertaining Distances at Sea, and a full Index.

List of Plates.

Plate I. Diagram Illustrative of the Triangulation. II. Specimen Page of Field Book. III. Running Survey of a Coast. IV. Example of a Running Survey from Belcher. V. Flying Survey of an Island. VI. Survey of a Shoal. VII. Boat Survey of a River. VIII. Three-Point Problem. IX. Triangulation.

Coffin's Navigation.

Fifth Edition.

12mo. Cloth. $3.50.

NAVIGATION AND NAUTICAL ASTRONOMY. Prepared for the use of the U. S. Naval Academy. By J. H. C. COFFIN, Prof. of Astronomy, Navigation and Surveying, with 52 woodcut illustrations.

Clark's Theoretical Navigation.

8vo. Cloth. $3.00.

THEORETICAL NAVIGATION AND NAUTICAL ASTRONOMY. By Lewis Clark, Lieut.-Commander, U. S. Navy. Illustrated with 41 Wood-cuts, including the Vernier.

Prepared for Use at the U. S. Naval Academy.

The Plane Table.

Illustrated. 8vo. Cloth. $2.00.

ITS USES IN TOPOGRAPHICAL SURVEYING. From the Papers of the U. S. Coast Survey.

This work gives a description of the Plane Table employed at the U. S. Coast Survey Office, and the manner of using it.

Pook on Shipbuilding.

8vo. Cloth. $5.00.

METHOD OF COMPARING THE LINES AND DRAUGHTING VESSELS PROPELLED BY SAIL OR STEAM, including a Chapter on Laying off on the Mould-Loft Floor. By Samuel M. Pook, Naval Constructor. 1 vol., 8vo. With illustrations. Cloth. $5.00.

Brunnow's Spherical Astronomy.

8vo. Cloth. $6.50.

SPHERICAL ASTRONOMY. By F. Brunnow, Ph. Dr. Translated by the Author from the Second German edition.

Van Buren's Formulas.

8vo. Cloth. $2.00.

INVESTIGATIONS OF FORMULAS, for the Strength of the Iron Parts of Steam Machinery. By J. D. VAN BUREN, JR., C. E. Illustrated.

This is an analytical discussion of the formulæ employed by mechanical engineers in determining the rupturing or crippling pressure in the different parts of a machine. The formulæ are founded upon the principle, that the different parts of a machine should be equally strong, and are developed in reference to the ultimate strength of the material in order to leave the choice of a factor of safety to the judgment of the designer.—*Silliman's Journal.*

Joynson on Machine Gearing.

8vo. Cloth. $2.00.

THE MECHANIC'S AND STUDENT'S GUIDE in the Designing and Construction of General Machine Gearing, as Eccentrics, Screws, Toothed Wheels, etc., and the Drawing of Rectilineal and Curved Surfaces ; with Practical Rules and Details. Edited by FRANCIS HERBERT JOYNSON. Illustrated with 18 folded plates.

"The aim of this work is to be a guide to mechanics in the designing and construction of general machine-gearing. This design it well fulfils, being plainly and sensibly written, and profusely illustrated."—*Sunday Times.*

Barnard's Report, Paris Exposition, 1867.

Illustrated. 8vo. Cloth. $5.00.

REPORT ON MACHINERY AND PROCESSES ON THE INDUSTRIAL ARTS AND APPARATUS OF THE EXACT SCIENCES. By F. A. P. BARNARD, LL.D.—Paris Universal Exposition, 1867.

"We have in this volume the results of Dr. Barnard's study of the Paris Exposition of 1867, in the form of an official Report of the Government. It is the most exhaustive treatise upon modern inventions that has appeared since the Universal Exhibition of 1851, and we doubt if anything equal to it has appeared this century."—*Journal Applied Chemistry.*

Engineering Facts and Figures.

18mo. Cloth. $2.50 per Volume.

AN ANNUAL REGISTER OF PROGRESS IN MECHANICAL ENGINEERING AND CONSTRUCTION, for the Years 1863–64–65–66–67–68. Fully illustrated. 6 volumes.

Each volume sold separately.

Beckwith's Pottery.

8vo. Paper. 60 cents.

OBSERVATIONS ON THE MATERIALS and Manufacture of Terra-Cotta, Stone-Ware, Fire-Brick, Porcelain and Encaustic Tiles, with Remarks on the Products exhibited at the London International Exhibition, 1871. By ARTHUR BECKWITH, Civil Engineer.

"Everything is noticed in this book which comes under the head of Pottery, from fine porcelain to ordinary brick, and aside from the interest which all take in such manufactures, the work will be of considerable value to followers of the ceramic art."—*Evening Mail.*

Dodd's Dictionary of Manufactures, etc.

12mo. Cloth. $2.00.

DICTIONARY OF MANUFACTURES, MINING, MACHINERY, AND THE INDUSTRIAL ARTS. By GEORGE DODD.

This work, a small book on a great subject, treats, in alphabetical arrangement, of those numerous matters which come generally within the range of manufactures and the productive arts. The raw materials—animal, vegetable, and mineral—whence the manufactured products are derived, are succinctly noticed in connection with the processes which they undergo, but not as subjects of natural history. The operations of the Mine and the Mill, the Foundry and the Forge, the Factory and the Workshop, are passed under review. The principal machines and engines, tools and apparatus, concerned in manufacturing processes, are briefly described. The scale on which our chief branches of national industry are conducted, in regard to values and quantities, is indicated in various ways.

Stuart's Civil and Military Engineering of America.

8vo. Illustrated. Cloth. $5.00.

THE CIVIL AND MILITARY ENGINEERS OF AMERICA. By General Charles B. Stuart, Author of "Naval Dry Docks of the United States," etc., etc. Embellished with nine finely executed portraits on steel of eminent engineers, and illustrated by engravings of some of the most important and original works constructed in America.

Containing sketches of the Life and Works of Major Andrew Ellicott, James Geddes (with Portrait), Benjamin Wright (with Portrait), Canvass White (with Portrait), David Stanhope Bates, Nathan S. Roberts, Gridley Bryant (with Portrait), General Joseph G. Swift, Jesse L. Williams (with Portrait), Colonel William McRee, Samuel H. Kneass, Captain John Childe (with Portrait), Frederick Harbach, Major David Bates Douglas (with Portrait), Jonathan Knight, Benjamin H. Latrobe (with Portrait), Colonel Charles Ellet, Jr. (with Portrait), Samuel Forrer, William Stuart Watson, John A. Roebling.

Alexander's Dictionary of Weights and Measures.

8vo. Cloth. $3.50.

UNIVERSAL DICTIONARY OF WEIGHTS AND MEASURES, Ancient and Modern, reduced to the standards of the United States of America. By J. H. Alexander. New edition. 1 vol.

"As a standard work of reference, this book should be in every library; it is one which we have long wanted, and it will save much trouble and research."—*Scientific American.*

Gouge on Ventilation.

Third Edition Enlarged.

8vo. Cloth. $2.00.

NEW SYSTEM OF VENTILATION, which has been thoroughly tested under the patronage of many distinguished persons. By Henry A. Gouge, with many illustrations.

Saeltzer's Acoustics.

12mo. Cloth. $2.00.

TREATISE ON ACOUSTICS in Connection with Ventilation. With a new theory based on an important discovery, of facilitating clear and intelligible sound in any building. By ALEXANDER SAELTZER.

"A practical and very sound treatise on a subject of great importance to architects, and one to which there has hitherto been entirly too little attention paid. The author's theory is, that, by bestowing proper care upon the point of Acoustics, the requisite ventilation will be obtained, and *vice versa.*—*Brooklyn Union.*

Myer's Manual of Signals.

New Edition. Enlarged.

12mo. 48 Plates full Roan. $5.00.

MANUAL OF SIGNALS, for the Use of Signal Officers in the Field, and for Military and Naval Students, Military Schools, etc. A new edition, enlarged and illustrated. By Brig.-Gen. ALBERT J. MYER, Chief Signal Officer of the Army, Colonel of the Signal Corps during the War of the Rebellion.

Larrabee's Secret Letter and Telegraph Code.

18mo. Cloth. $1.00.

CIPHER AND SECRET LETTER AND TELEGRAPHIC CODE, with Hogg's Improvements. The most perfect secret Code ever invented or discovered. Impossible to read without the Key. Invaluable for Secret, Military, Naval, and Diplomatic Service, as well as for Brokers, Bankers, and Merchants. By C. S. LARRABEE, the original inventor of the scheme.

Hunt's Designs for Central Park Gateways.

4to. Cloth. $5.00.

DESIGNS FOR THE GATEWAYS OF THE SOUTHERN ENTRANCES TO THE CENTRAL PARK. By Richard M. Hunt. With a description of the designs.

Pickert and Metcalf's Art of Graining.

1 vol. 4to. Cloth. $10.00.

THE ART OF GRAINING. How Acquired and How Produced, with description of colors and their application. By Charles Pickert and Abraham Metcalf. Beautifully illustrated with 42 tinted plates of the various woods used in interior finishing. Tinted paper.

The authors present here the result of long experience in the practice of this decorative art, and feel confident that they hereby offer to their brother artisans a reliable guide to improvement in the practice of graining.

Portrait Gallery of the War.

60 fine Portraits on Steel. Royal 8vo. Cloth. $6.00.

PORTRAIT GALLERY OF THE WAR, CIVIL, MILITARY AND NAVAL. A Biographical Record. Edited by Frank Moore.

One Law in Nature.

12mo. Cloth. $1.50.

ONE LAW IN NATURE. By Capt. H. M. Lazelle, U. S. A. A New Corpuscular Theory, comprehending Unity of Force, Identity of Matter, and its Multiple Atom Constitution, applied to the Physical Affections or Modes of Energy.

Ernst's Manual of Military Engineering.

193 Wood Cuts and 3 Lithographed Plates. 12mo. Cloth. $5.00.

A MANUAL OF PRACTICAL MILITARY ENGINEERING. Prepared for the use of the Cadets of the U. S. Military Academy, and for Engineer Troops. By Capt. O. H. ERNST, Corps of Engineers, Instructor in Practical Military Engineering, U. S. Military Academy.

Church's Metallurgical Journey.

24 Illustrations. 8vo. Cloth. $2.00.

NOTES OF A METALLURGICAL JOURNEY IN EUROPE. By JOHN A. CHURCH, Engineer of Mines.

Blake's Precious Metals.

8vo. Cloth. $2.00.

REPORT UPON THE PRECIOUS METALS: Being Statistical Notices of the principal Gold and Silver producing regions of the World. Represented at the Paris Universal Exposition. By WILLIAM P. BLAKE, Commissioner from the State of California.

Clevenger's Surveying.

Illustrated Pocket Form. Morocco Gilt. $2.50.

A TREATISE ON THE METHOD OF GOVERNMENT SURVEYING, as prescribed by the United States Congress. and Commissioner of the General Land Office. With complete Mathematical, Astronomical and Practical Instructions, for the use of the United States Surveyors in the Field, and Students who contemplate engaging in the business of Public Land Surveying. By S. R. CLEVENGER, U. S. Deputy Surveyor.

"The reputation of the author as a surveyor guarantees an exhaustive treatise on this subject."—*Dakota Register.*

"Surveyors have long needed a text-book of this description.—*The Press.*

SILVER MINING REGIONS OF COLORADO, with some account of the different Processes now being introduced for working the Gold Ores of that Territory. By J. P. WHITNEY. 12mo. Paper. 25 cents.

COLORADO: SCHEDULE OF ORES contributed by sundry persons to the Paris Universal Exposition of 1867, with some information about the Region and its Resources. By J. P. WHITNEY, Commissioner from the Territory. 8vo. Paper, with Maps. 25 cents.

THE SILVER DISTRICTS OF NEVADA. With Map. 8vo. Paper. 35 cents.

ARIZONA: ITS RESOURCES AND PROSPECTS. By Hon. R. C. McCORMICK, Secretary of the Territory. With Map. 8vo. Paper. 25 cents.

MONTANA AS IT IS. Being a general description of its Resources, both Mineral and Agricultural; including a complete description of the face of the country, its climate, etc. Illustrated with a Map of the Territory, showing the different Roads and the location of the different Mining Districts. To which is appended a complete Dictionary of THE SNAKE LANGUAGE, and also of the famous Chinnook Jargon, with numerous critical and explanatory Notes. By GRANVILLE STUART. 8vo. Paper. $2.00.

RAILWAY GAUGES. A Review of the Theory of Narrow Gauges as applied to Main Trunk Lines of Railway. By SILAS SEYMOUR, Genl. Consulting Engineer. 8vo. Paper. 50 cents.

REPORT made to the President and Executive Board of the Texas Pacific Railroad. By Gen. G. P. BUELL, Chief Engineer. 8vo. Paper. 75 cents.

Van Nostrand's Science Series.

It is the intention of the Publisher of this Series to issue them at intervals of about a month. They will be put up in a uniform, neat and attractive form, 18mo, fancy boards. The subjects will be of an eminently scientific character, and embrace as wide a range of topics as possible, all of the highest character.

Price, 50 Cents Each.

1.

CHIMNEYS FOR FURNACES, FIRE-PLACES, AND STEAM BOILERS. By R. Armstrong, C. E.

2.

STEAM BOILER EXPLOSIONS. By Zerah Colburn.

3.

PRACTICAL DESIGNING OF RETAINING WALLS By Arthur Jacob, A. B. With Illustrations.

4.

PROPORTIONS OF PINS USED IN BRIDGES. By Charles E. Bender, C. E. With Illustrations.

5.

VENTILATION OF BUILDINGS. By W. F. Butler. With Illustrations.

6.

ON THE DESIGNING AND CONSTRUCTION OF STORAGE RESERVOIRS. By Arthur Jacob. With Illustrations.

7.

SURCHARGED AND DIFFERENT FORMS OF RETAINING WALLS. By James S. Tate, C. E.

8.

A TREATISE ON THE COMPOUND ENGINE. By John Turnbull. With Illustrations.

9.

FUEL. By C. W. Siemens to which is appended the Value of Artificial Fuels as compared with Coal. By J. Wormald, C. E.

*** Other works in preparation.

www.ingramcontent.com/pod-product-compliance
Lightning Source LLC
LaVergne TN
LVHW021425110826
845150LV00007B/2089
9781425507909